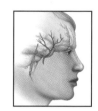

Critical Decisions in
Headache
Management

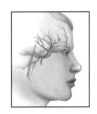

Critical Decisions in
Headache
Management

Rose Giammarco, M.D.
McMaster University
Hamilton, Ontario

John Edmeads, M.D.
University of Toronto
Toronto, Ontario

David Dodick, M.D.
Mayo Clinic
Rochester, Minnesota

1998
B.C. Decker Inc.
Hamilton • London

B.C. Decker Inc.
4 Hughson Street South
P.O. Box 620, L.C.D. 1
Hamilton, Ontario, Canada L8N 3K7
Tel: 905-522-7017
Fax: 905-522-7839
e-mail: info@bcdecker.com

97 98 99 00 01 / BP / 9 8 7 6 5 4 3 2 1

ISBN 1-55009-029-1
Printed in Canada

Sales and Distribution

United States
Blackwell Science Inc.
Commerce Place, 350 Main Street
Malden, MA 02148, U.S.A.
Tel: 800-215-1000

Canada
Copp Clark Ltd.
200 Adelaide Street West, 3rd Floor
Toronto, Ontario, Canada M5H 1W7
Tel: 416-597-1616
Fax: 416-597-1617

Japan
Igaku-Shoin Ltd.
Tokyo, International P.O. Box 5063
1-28-36 Hongo, Bunkyo-ku, Tokyo 113, Japan
Tel: 3 3817-5680
Fax: 3 3815-7805

U.K., Europe, Scandinavia, Middle East
Blackwell Science Ltd.
c/o Marston Book Services Ltd.
P.O. Box 87, Oxford OX2 0DT, England
Tel: 44-1865-79115

Australia
Blackwell Science Pty, Ltd.
54 University Street
Carlton, Victoria 3053, Australia
Tel: 03 9347 0300
Fax: 03 9349 3016

India
Jaypee Brothers Medical Publishers Ltd.
B-3, Emca House, 23/23B, Ansari Road, Daryaganj,
P.B. 7193, New Delhi - 110002, India
Tel: 11 3272143
Fax: 11 3272143

CONTENTS

PREFACE

Headache is among the most common presenting medical complaints. An accurate headache diagnosis, which is in large part dependent on a careful history, is essential for successful patient management.

Critical Decisions in Headache Management presents the clinical process of assessing and treating the headache patient in the office and hospital settings, including adults and children, acute and chronic sufferers, routine and challenging patients. The work is intended to complement the principal texts and reference works on headache, and to illustrate how to employ the information they contain. Our goal is to construct decision trees that demonstrate critical decision points clearly and are simple to follow. The comments are keyed to designated decision nodes to elaborate a principle or provide background support, and selected references allow the motivated reader to dig a little deeper.

We are indebted to several talented individuals in putting this work together. David Mazierski's original illustrations are a perfect complement to the written work; Anne McKibbon's Introduction and 32 Search Strategies provide the reader with keys to the modern electronic library. To our knowledge, the feature is unique in the book literature. Janette Lush and Jennifer Sullivan at B.C. Decker have visited on the production and editing process both skill and loving care. To these people we express our grateful admiration.

Dr. Julian Dobranowski contributed the images to the radiology chapter, and reviewed the text of this unit. The pediatrics chapter was reviewed by Dr. Gabriella DeVeber. To both of them we express our thanks. Nonetheless, any errors or omissions in the work are our responsibility.

We hope that students will find the book a useful introduction to the subject of headache diagnosis and management, and that the already initiated will consider it a refreshing means of reviewing the topic.

Rose Giammarco
John Edmeads
David Dodick
June, 1997

INTRODUCTION TO SEARCH STRATEGIES

The pace at which new health information evolves presents a challenge for health care professionals trying to keep abreast of new developments in health care. The Internet has become an effective tool for keeping current, but it presents a further challenge in identifying what is important and scientifically sound for clinicians, patients, and advocates to use. One of the biggest benefits of publishing information using the Internet is the ease of updating documents – a new edition can be published in an afternoon.

In this book, we introduce a mechanism that allows the reader to supplement the bibliographies in this book with current changes in headache management. Each chapter of the book contains its own MEDLINE search strategy, which can be used to find more information on the topic, or any newly published information.

The MEDLINE database is used as the starting point for finding information, because it is the database containing much of the information on headaches, and because most health care professionals can access the database. MEDLINE is a bibliographic database that includes 8 million citations, dating back to 1966, culled from more than 4000 health-related journals.

Many MEDLINE systems exist, each with their own searching programs and peculiarities. Two good listings of searching systems are on the Internet, and can be found at the following internet addresses:

http://www.medlib.iupui.edu/ref/drfelix-mirror.html
http://www.medmatrix.org/SPages/Medline.stm

We have chosen to use Windows Grateful Med as our "presentation system" because it clearly illustrates many of the searching features used in the search strategies for this book. Most of the systems accessible by health care professionals will be able to use these searching features. If you have difficulty "translating" our strategies into your searching system, consult your librarian or systems staff, or use the manual.

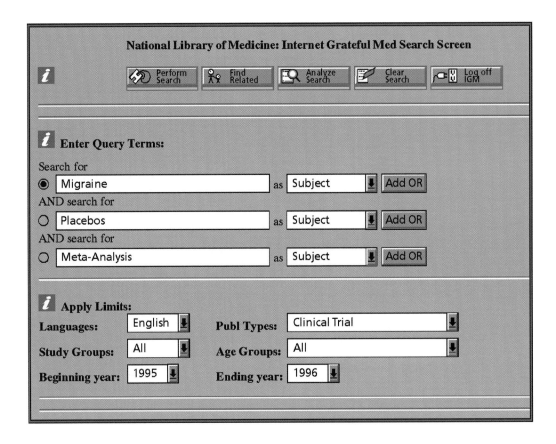

In the "explode" feature, information is indexed in a hierarchical manner, e.g., a newborn is also (or a subset of) an infant or a child. The "explode" feature allows the "gathering" or collecting of similar terms. For example, "explode heart valves" collects material on aortic, mitral, pulmonary and papillary muscles. "Explode sports" would include 24 activities, from baseball to wrestling. Note that not all systems require you to explode your terms; again, check with other experts or your systems manual.

Two examples of search strategies follow; one searching for information on the history of headaches, and the other searching for information on clinical trials of drug therapy for cluster headaches.

Supplementary Search Strategy (SuSS)
(**sus** or **suss** n. & v.t. (sl.) suspect; suspicion; ~**out**, reconnoiter.)

History of headaches (retrieval is approximately 20 citations)

SuSS I	
Subject	Headache (index term)
History	History (text word)
Limited to	1994 through 1997

Drug therapy for cluster headaches (retrieval is approximately 15 citations)

SuSS I	
Subject	Cluster headache (index term)
Subject	Drug therapy (text word)
Limit to	Human (publication type)
AND	Meta-analysis (publication type) or Clinical Trial (publication type)
AND	1994 through 1997

We hope this device helps you to "SuSS" out additional sources from the literature.

Because this is the first time we have incorporated search strategies into a book, we welcome your feedback.

Chapter 1

HEADACHE IN HISTORY

The practice of medicine is a rational endeavor in which the cause of a disease is identified and then treatment aimed at correcting that cause is applied. It was always so. In the Stone Age, illness was inflicted by supernatural beings, and treatment was magical. In the Space Age, molecular disturbances cause bodily dysfunction and are corrected through receptor pharmacology. Headache treatment, and in particular the management of migraine, provides a dramatic example of this progress in medicine from magic to molecules.

ANCIENT HEADACHE THERAPY

In most civilizations of the ancient era, including those of Mesopotamia, Egypt, India, and early Greece, headaches were believed to be caused by malevolent beings who either themselves occupied the cranium of the sufferer or implanted the "headache" as an entity into the head. Appropriate treatment by the priest-physicians of the day was aimed at appeasing the responsible spirit by offering prayers to it or applying valued items to the head. Also, they tried to exorcise the headache by appeals to the more powerful and beneficent deities or by adorning the head with repulsive substances.

Several regimens incorporated these therapeutic principles. For example, a 7000-year-old Sumerian headache remedy advised the following:

> Take the hair of a virgin kid, and let a skilled woman spin it on the right side, then double it on the left and tie it in twice seven knots. Bless it with the incantation of Eridu, and with it bind the head. Cast water over the sick man, so that the headache may ascend to heaven.

An Egyptian papyrus dating from about 2500 B.C. suggested a similar regimen:

> The physician shall take a crocodile made of clay, with an eye of faience, and straw in its mouth, and bind it on the head using a strip of fine linen upon which have been written the names of the Gods ... and the physician shall pray.

Figure 1.1 Egyptian papyrus dating to about 2500 B.C., found in a temple in Thebes. It is part of a medical treatise, and deals with the treatment of headache.

Figure 1.2 This is an illustration which translates the papyrus in Figure 1 as follows: "The physician shall take a crocodile of clay, with an eye of faience and straw in its mouth, and shall fasten it to the head of the sufferer with a strip of fine linen upon which has been written the names of the Gods ... and the physician shall pray." Have we really progressed all that far?

These treatments were likely effective, for they were espoused by two different cultures separated by thousands of miles and thousands of years. Why did they work? Perhaps binding the head collapsed painfully distended scalp vessels, relieving vascular headache. Certainly head-binding has always been a widely employed lay remedy for headache; recall that Shakespeare has Desdemona, upon hearing Othello, complain, "I have a pain upon my forehead here," produce a handkerchief and say, "Faith, that's with watching; 'twill away again: let me but bind it hard, within this hour it will be well." Placebo response was also a likely mechanism; relief of pain from placebo occurs in up to a third of headache patients, and a treatment based on a belief system that permeated the culture might have had even more powerful placebo properties.

The Ayurvedic medical tradition of ancient India was based on the tenet that illness was caused by divine punishment, but some beneficent gods did teach the priestly sages the use of medicines to mitigate this punishment. Among these medications was Rauwolfia serpentina, which was prized for its potency in the treatment of snakebite, agitation, and headache. In its present form, reserpine may with chronic dosing worsen migraine, probably via its activity in depleting serotonin and other biogenic amines. However, one can speculate that it might have relieved those headaches associated with severe hypertension or chronic anxiety.

In early Greece also, illness was considered the work of the gods, but with the advent of the school of Thales in approximately 600 B.C., there developed a new approach: an attempt to ascribe all phenomena to natural rather than supernatural causes. Hippocrates (approximately 400 B.C.) believed that headaches were attributable to an imbalance of the elements with a rise of humors to the head; he recommended bleeding (presumably to drain or reverse the flow of the humors) followed by the application of herbs such as hellebore to the head. Galen, the Roman medical authority (A.D. 150) who based much of his system of medicine on the teaching of Hippocrates, purged patients with headaches, presumably to rid the body of noxious substances by another route. It seems paradoxical that the therapeutic regimens produced by the shift of medical theory from supernatural to natural realms became, if anything, less effective and more potentially harmful than the treatments based on magic.

MEDIEVAL HEADACHE THERAPY

Medicine in the Middle Ages, though separated from the priesthood, was no less authoritarian and dogmatic than it had been when diagnosis and treatment were handed down by the gods. Secular physicians followed rigidly the therapeutic precepts laid down by previous generations. For example, the following regimen, written around A.D. 800 in the medical text *Incipit Epistula Vulturus*, was still in use half a millennium later:

> The bones from the head of the vulture, wrapped in deerskin, will cure any headache; its brain, mixed with the best of oil and put up the nose, will expel all ailments of the head.

Medieval Arabian physicians employed equally vigorous therapy for headache; for example, Abulcasis (around A.D. 1000) advocated the application of a red-hot poker to the forehead, or cutting the temple with a knife and rubbing garlic into the incision. These treatments were used widely and for many centuries, suggesting that they must have had some efficacy. Likely, placebo effect was responsible, though it may also have been that wise headache sufferers stopped complaining for fear that the treatment, if found unsuccessful the first time, might be repeated.

There were some kinder methods in use. In thirteenth century Italy a medical manuscript recommended that a cloth soaked in vinegar and opium be applied to the forehead. Acetic acid may enhance transcutaneous absorption, and conceivably some of the opium could have been assimilated through the skin.

When the European explorers of the fifteenth and sixteenth centuries discovered the New World, they found systems of medicine in use that were not dissimilar to those of the Old World. The Incas incised the scalp when treating headache,

Figure 1.3 Pre-Columbian surgical instrument found in Central America. The semicircular blade at the bottom was used to cut holes in the skull. The vertical part is the handle, and on the top of the handle is carved a tableau with three figures ... patient, nurse, and surgeon ... showing the surgeon how to use the instrument. Presumably, surgeons were illiterate in those days. The presumption (unproven) is that instruments such as these were used to cut holes in people's heads to release evil spirits that might be causing headaches and other neuromaladies.

and dripped the juice of the cocoa leaf into the wound (one wonders if the local anesthetic properties of cocaine played a role in the efficacy of this treatment). Trephination was widely practiced by the Incas and the Tumi, sometimes with survival, for pre-Columbian skulls have been found in Peru with evidence of healing. The purpose of the trephination is not known; in particular we do not know if it was used for headache, though certainly it was used, rarely, in seventeenth century Europe as a headache treatment (*vide infra*).

In North America local treatment of the head for headache was widely practiced by many tribes. The Chippewa affixed quills to a piece of wood and used this instrument to apply to the forehead, by scarification, the juice of the painted trillium. In resistant cases the dried gall of a bear was mixed with charcoal and applied with this instrument to the temple, leaving dark blotches on the skin of some Indians, which identified them as headache sufferers. Presumably it was the trauma to the head that was effective, rather than what substance was applied, for some tribes used scarification alone. In July, 1609, Samuel de Champlain was leading a raiding party of 60 Montagnais, Algonquins, and Hurons into Iroquois territory when, on the shores of what was to become known as Lake Champlain, his companions caught a pike. He recorded:

> The natives give me the head, a thing they prize highly, saying that when they have a headache, they bleed themselves with the teeth of these fish at the spot where the pain is and it eases them at once.

Clearly this treatment worked; Champlain carried the head of the pike with him, and when he returned to France on October 13, 1609, he presented it to King Henry IV at Fontainebleau.

MIGRAINE TREATMENT IN THE RENAISSANCE

In seventeenth century Europe migraine was becoming distinguishable from other types of headache, largely because of the classic descriptions of the condition by the master clinician, Thomas Willis. Willis had also enunciated a new explanation for migraine, that it was caused by distention of the blood vessels of the head, which led to treatment by local removal of the blood from the head (not unlike the treatment demonstrated to Champlain half a century earlier). Sometimes simple incision of the temple was done. The practice in Holland was to place a heated glass globe over the incision, and as the globe cooled, a vacuum was established that aspirated the blood. In this way several patients could be treated at once, similar to some of the headache clinics of today. The systemic venesection recommended by Hippocrates was also employed to reduce the pressure of the blood within the head. A good example of Renaissance treatment of the difficult migraine patient was provided by Willis's account of his problem patient Anne, Countess Conway. He treated her "megrim" once by temporal arteriotomy, on several occasions by venesections, and on occasion with mercurials (to provoke salivation, though we can only speculate on how this was seen to help the headache). She obtained a second opinion from William Harvey, who recommended that she attend a French surgeon for trephination in order to release pressure from the head. Willis recorded:

Figure 1.4 Portrait of Thomas Willis. The 17th century English physician gave us classical descriptions of migraine and first enunciated the vascular theory of migraine. The circle of Willis is his eponymous contribution to vascular anatomy.

> There remains yet another chirurgical operation, extoll'd by many for an obstinate Headach, but tryed as yet by none that I know, to wit, the opening of the Scull with a trepand Iron near the place of the pain. Our famous Harvey endeavour'd to perswade a Lady of great quality to this, who was troubled with a terrible and inveterate head-ach, promising her a Cure therebye; but neither she nor any other has been content to admit of the administration. Truly it does not appear to me what certainty we may expect from the Scull being opened where it pains.

Other Renaissance treatments included the application, to the head and elsewhere, of various fomentations and "plaisters," purging, and the systematic administration of herbs. Opium was prescribed, but the oral route and the low potency of the preparations available likely prevented efficacy.

Momentous advances in the understanding of the pathophysiology of migraine in the Renaissance were not mirrored by similar advances in treatment. The therapy of migraine remained tradition-bound, largely ineffective, and sometimes dangerous.

Figure 1.5 Swedish painting, 17th century, artist unknown. A surgeon of the day is incising a scalp artery in the patient in an attempt to relieve the pain of headache.

VICTORIAN ERA

With the nineteenth century came increasing emphasis on science in medicine, on the need to verify belief with observation, and on critical evaluation of therapeutic practices. Treatments were prescribed only if they could be shown to be effective, a phenomenon that trashed the traditional pharmacopeia and introduced a new, leaner one. Headache treatment was almost exclusively pharmacologic, and the number of medications available was small. Romberg, author of the major European neurology text of the day (1853), proclaimed in his chapter on "Neuralgia Cerebralis … Hemicrania":

> In our treatment … we cannot be sufficiently on our guard against the abuse of medicine. During the attack, the recumbent position, with the head raised, affords relief which is also promoted by darkening the room, by quietude, and by giving tepid tea to assist the vomiting … Remedies applied to head externally are unnecessary. The local abstraction of blood is to be avoided.

Gowers, in his classic English textbook of 1888, emphasized the importance of first removing "any error in mode of life or defect in general health." He distinguished carefully between preventive medication, aimed at "rendering the attacks less frequent and less severe" and ad hoc treatment of the attack itself. Gowers felt that nitroglycerine given regularly two or three times a day, after food, could have "a striking effect in many patients, rendering the attacks far slighter and far less frequent, and occasionally stopping them altogether." It is difficult to see how a vasodilating drug could help migraine, and equally difficult to believe that an experienced and critical clinician like Gowers would endorse an inefficacious treatment. Given that Gowers recommended small doses (0.3 mg) by mouth on a full stomach, and cautioned specifically against giving more, or in the fasting state, it may be that some tolerance or desensitization to vasodilatation was slowly being achieved. Gowers hypothesized that "It is possible that the drug acts chiefly by periodically flushing the nerve centers with arterial blood, and so improving the nutrition and function of the nerve cells." For those resistant to nitroglycerine he proposed chronic dosing with bromide, a therapy that might have worked by virtue of its sedative effect.

For treatment of the acute attack, Gowers advocated higher doses of bromide (1.8 to 2.4 g), often in combination with a tincture of Indian hemp (cannabis). Chloral he found less efficacious, but a "hypodermic injection of morphia … occasionally gives great relief." He felt that "ergotin" was of little value (possibly because this primitive compound of mixed ergot alkaloids was of low potency). Osler's

(1892) preferred treatment for the acute attack of migraine was cannabis, though he found that taken early in the attack, phenacetin and antipyrine could be useful.

The treatment advocated by the great Victorian clinicians was not dramatic, and at times was ineffective; however, their conservatism and their demand that the true test of therapy be its efficacy and not its ancestry provided an essential "stable-sweeping" that cleared the way for the momentous therapeutic advances of the twentieth century.

TWENTIETH CENTURY

Headache treatment today has been shaped by (a) better understanding of the pathophysiology of migraine; (b) the increasing ability of pharmacologists to design and manufacture drugs to correct the observed physiologic dysfunctions; and (c) the rigorous testing of drugs in a controlled fashion to establish efficacy. These abilities and techniques are hard won. In the early years of this century, advances were slow, as typified by the development of ergotamine.

Given the theory that migraine headache was caused by cranial vasodilatation, and given the observed vasospastic properties of the fungus ergot, clinicians used crude aqueous extracts of this fungus for headache treatment as early as 1868, but, as noted by Gowers 20 years later, this "ergotin" was of inconsistent benefit. In 1925 Rothlin isolated the potent alkaloid ergotamine, and this was introduced into migraine treatment later that year by Maier, becoming more widely used after that because of its demonstrated efficacy. It is a commentary on the regulatory climate of the time that the laboratory study which showed that ergotamine actually did constrict the scalp vessels was not done until 1938. Not until some years later were many of the beneficial and adverse aspects of ergotamine appreciated. For example, it was not until the early 1980s that the efficacy of dihydroergotamine (DHE) in treating chronic daily headaches was discovered; paradoxically, it was not until about the same time that it became apparent that overuse of ergotamine could cause chronic daily headache.

The vagaries of headache pharmacology are further illustrated by the development in 1958 of the migraine prophylactic medication, methysergide. This molecule was synthesized as a serotonin antagonist, working on the belief, then current, that migraine was caused by an excess of serotonin. Subsequent studies showing a deficiency of serotonin in migraine made it difficult to explain the effectiveness of methysergide. Thirty years later it became clear that there were different types of serotonin receptors, that methysergide probably exerted its prophylactic effect by blocking one type (the 5-HT$_2$ receptor), and that medication useful for the acute attack worked by stimulating another (the 5-HT$_1$ receptor).

These advances in pharmacology have produced parallel advances in migraine therapy, as exemplified by the development of the drug sumatriptan for the treatment of the acute attack of migraine. This is a true "designer drug," synthesized to combine with and stimulate only the 5-HT$_{1D}$ receptors, thus constricting the dilated cranial vessels without, through combining with other types of receptors, producing side effects. The significance of sumatriptan is not so much that it is another effective treatment for the acute attack of migraine (which it is), but that it exemplifies the new, rational, and powerful pharmacologic approach of tailor-making drugs to act solely on a specific receptor. It is a harbinger of many things to come.

Meanwhile, on a more mundane level, serendipity has played a continuing role in the adoption of drugs for the treatment of migraine. The most familiar example is the observation in 1966 during a study of angina pectoris that the regular ingestion of propranolol reduced the frequency of migraine attacks. This observation has been verified in numerous controlled studies, and propranolol has become the most widely prescribed prophylactic medication for migraine, despite the fact that, a quarter of a century later, no one can explain how or why it works. Other examples of the serendipitous discovery of migraine prophylactic efficacy in drugs developed for other indications are verapamil, amitriptyline, and valproic acid. These discoveries are valuable not only because they have provided effective treatment for migraine, but perhaps more so because they ask questions that, when answered, may throw new light on the pathogenesis of migraine.

OVERVIEW

Migraine has been a problem and a challenge for patients and physicians for over 7000 years. As with medicine in general, the management of migraine has moved from the temple to the clinic and the laboratory, and specific treatment has left the realm of magic and entered the age of molecular biology. The startling progress in migraine management over the past decade augurs well for the headache sufferer.

Bibliography

Armstrong JCW. Champlain. Toronto: Macmillan, 1987:109–114.

Beecher H. The powerful placebo. JAMA 1955; 159:1602–1606.

Critchley M. Migraine from Cappadocia to Queen Square. In: Smith R, ed. Background to migraine. London: W Heinemann, 1967:28–38.

Edmeads J. Bringing treatment to a head. Headache 1991; 31:695.

Edmeads J. Treating the head in headache. Headache 1988; 28:496–497.

Friedman AP. The headache in history, literature and legend. Bull NY Acad Med 1972; 48:661–681.

Gowers WR. A manual of diseases of the nervous system. Philadelphia: P Blakiston, Son & Co., 1888:1187–1188. (Reprinted in facsimile by The Classics of Neurology & Neurosurgery Library, Birmingham, Alabama: Gryphon Editions, 1983.)

Graham JR, Wolff HG. Mechanisms of migraine headache and action of ergotamine tartrate. Arch Neurol Psychiatry 1938; 39:737–763.

Humphrey PPA, Feniuk W, Perren MJ. Anti-migraine drugs in development: advances in serotonin receptor pharmacology. Headache 1990; 30:12–16.

Lyons AS, Petrucelli RJ. Medicine, an illustrated history. New York: Harry N Abrams Inc, 1978:113–115.

MacKinney IC. An unpublished treatise on medicine and magic from the age of Charlemagne. Speculum 1943; 18:494–496.

Osler W. The principles and practice of medicine. New York: D. Appleton and Company, 1892:959. (Reprinted in facsimile by The Classics of Medicine Library, Birmingham, Alabama: Gryphon Editions, 1978.)

Papyrus number 10685, verso 4. Section of Egyptology. The British Museum. London, England.

Peroutka SJ. The pharmacology of current anti-migraine drugs. Headache 1990; 30:5–11.

Rabkin R, Stables DP, Levin NW, et al. The prophylactic value of propranolol in angina pectoris. Am J Cardiol 1966; 18:370–380.

Romberg MH. A manual of the nervous diseases of man. (Translated by Sievekin EH). London: The Sydenham Society, 1853:177. (Reprinted in facsimile by The Classics of Neurology & Neurosurgery Library, Birmingham, Alabama: Gryphon Editions, 1983.)

Shakespeare W. Othello. Act 3, scene 3, lines 326–329 (New Folger Library edition, 1993).

Willis T. The London practice of physick. London: Basset and Crooke, 1685:380. (Reprinted in facsimile by The Classics of Neurology & Neurosurgery Library, Birmingham, Alabama: Gryphon Editions, 1991.)

Supplementary Search Strategy

SuSS I	
Subject	Headache (index term)
History	History (subheading)
Limited to	1994 through 1997

Chapter 2

CLASSIFICATION OF HEADACHE

Why classify? First, classification is a method of ordering our knowledge that makes it more understandable, more memorable, and more accessible. Second, a logical classification, especially if simple and brief, can be of great clinical use.

Recall (see Chapter 1) that before 400 B.C. headache was considered to be a *morbus sui generis,* a disease unto itself. Not until Hippocrates classified headaches into those that were secondary to other diseases (such as meningitis) and those that were primary (such as migraine), did diagnosis begin to make any sense; and not until diagnosis became comprehensible did treatment begin to be rational. The classification of headaches has evolved in fits and starts ever since, with tension-type headaches being separated out from the vast motley of "not secondary, but not migraine" headaches at the end of the nineteenth century, and cluster headaches being recognized as a specific primary headache in the 1930s.

Present-day classifications retain the distinction between "primary headaches" (such as migraine, tension-type headaches, cluster headaches, and other less common types) and "secondary headaches" (such as those associated with brain tumors, sinusitis, vasculitis, and the like). The more useful classifications incorporate descriptions of the various types; when these descriptions are sufficiently rigorous, they become diagnostic criteria.

The headache classification most widely accepted today is that of the International Headache Society (IHS), entitled "Classification and Diagnostic Criteria for Headache Disorders, Cranial Neuralgias and Facial Pain" (1988). It was originally designed for the use of headache researchers, and thus is authoritative, complex, and comprehensive. It is also 97 pages long. Most clinicians, particularly those who are not headache experts, do not use the IHS classification in its original form, but instead employ the briefer and simpler modifications. Table 2.1 is one of these modifications.

Table 2.1   Types of Headaches

Migraine

Migraine without aura ("common migraine")

Migraine with aura
- migraine with typical aura ("classical migraine")
- migraine with atypical aura (several rare types including basilar migraine and hemiplegic migraine)

Ophthalmoplegic migraine

Complications of migraine
- migraine associated with stroke
- prolonged migraine attack ("status migrainosus")

Childhood migraine equivalents
- recurrent episodes of abdominal pain/vomiting
- benign paroxysmal vertigo

Tension-type headache

Episodic tension-type headache
- with evidence of scalp/neck muscle involvement
- without evidence of muscle involvement

Chronic or continuous tension-type headache
- with evidence of scalp/neck muscle involvement
- without evidence of muscle involvement

Cluster headache and chronic paroxysmal hemicrania

Episodic cluster headache (occurring in discrete cycles)
Chronic cluster headaches (not occurring in discrete cycles)
Chronic paroxysmal hemicrania

Miscellaneous benign dysfunctional headaches

Includes ice-pick headaches, ice cream headaches, cough headaches, exertional headaches, sexual headaches ("coital cephalalgia"), and so on

Post-traumatic headaches

Headache associated with vascular diseases

Atherosclerotic or embolic cerebrovascular disease
Intracranial hematoma (parenchymal or dural)
Subarachnoid hemorrhage

Vasculitides
- giant cell ("temporal") arteritis

Arterial dissections

Intracranial venous thrombosis

Unruptured arteriovenous malformations
- parenchymal
- dural

Table 2.1 Continued

Headache from other intracranial diseases

Altered cerebrospinal fluid (CSF) pressure
- high CSF pressure syndromes such as "benign" intracranial hypertension and hydrocephalus
- low CSF pressure syndromes such as postlumbar puncture (LP) headaches and CSF fistulae

Intracranial mass lesions
- neoplasms
- others

Intracranial inflammation
- infections, such as meningitis, brain abscess
- noninfective inflammations such as sarcoidosis

Headaches associated with substances or their withdrawal

Acute use or exposure
- nitrates, monosodium glutamate (MSG), CO, alcohol, others

Chronic use or exposure
- ergotamine, analgesic, or benzodiazepine abuse
- H_2 blockers, some nonsteroidal anti-inflammatory drugs (NSAIDs), some antibiotics, etc.

Withdrawal
- from alcohol, ergotamine, analgesics, caffeine, etc.

Headaches associated with systemic (noncephalic) infections

Headaches associated with metabolic disorders

Hypoxia
Hypercarbia
Hypoglycemia
Dialysis

Headaches associated with diseases of the skull, neck, eyes, sinuses

Cranial neuralgias

Trigeminal neuralgia (tic douloureux)
Occipital neuralgia
Glossopharyngeal and other rare cranial neuralgias
Herpes zoster of V_1
Tolosa-Hunt syndrome

The IHS classification assigns to each of these 12 main headache types, and to most of their subtypes, specific criteria to be met if these entities are to be diagnosed. Rather than replicate all of these here, Tables 2.2 to 2.4 display, as examples, how the classification works, the diagnostic criteria, shortened and simplified, for migraine without aura, episodic tension-type headache, and low cerebrospinal fluid pressure headaches. Note how the criteria give considerable guidance about which features to seek out on history and examination, and which investigations to do.

Table 2.2   Diagnostic Criteria for Migraine Without Aura

A. Multiple* attacks of headaches fulfilling criteria B to D
B. Headaches last a few hours to a few days each [†]
C. Headache has at least two of the following characteristics:
  • unilaterality
  • pulsatility
  • intensity great enough to affect normal daily activities [‡]
  • headache aggravated by routine physical activity such as climbing stairs
D. Headache is accompanied by at least one of:
  • nausea and/or vomiting
  • hypersensitivity to noise, light, and/or smells [§]
E. No evidence on history or examination of any other disorder which could be causing the headaches

*What does "multiple" mean? The IHS classification demands "at least 5 attacks." This is rather rigid. The main thing is that migraine is a **recurrent** disorder. If a patient has just two or three attacks that are typical, it is migraine.

[†] The IHS classification demands that each attack lasts "4–72 hours." Again, this is a bit rigid. If the attack is otherwise typical and lasts 2 hours, or 80 hours, it is migraine.

[‡] The IHS classification refers to "moderate or severe intensity," but immediately expands on this by defining it as intensity sufficient to inhibit or prohibit daily activities. Note, incidentally, that it is possible (though not common) to have a mild migraine attack.

[§] The IHS classification does not refer to osmophobia, or hypersensitivity to smells, during attacks, but it is common, fairly specific, and therefore a clinically useful criterion.

Table 2.3   Diagnostic Criteria for Episodic Tension-type Headache *

A. Multiple attacks of headaches with the following characteristics
B. Headaches last half an hour to a week each
C. Headache has at least two of the following attributes:
  • bilateral
  • nonpulsatile
  • no more than moderate intensity, insufficient to prevent activity
  • not aggravated by routine physical activity
D. Headache not accompanied by anything or, at most by a little hypersensitivity to noise or light
E. No evidence on history or examination of any other disorder which could be causing the headaches

* Note what a nondescript headache this is. Essentially, it is an episodic, mild-to-moderate headache that is not migraine. This goes along with our near-total ignorance of the pathophysiology of tension-type headache.

Table 2.4 Diagnostic Criteria for Low Cerebrospinal Fluid Pressure Headaches

Postlumbar Puncture Headache
A. Bilateral headache developed less than 7 days after lumbar puncture
B. Headache occurs or worsens less than 15 minutes after assuming upright position, and disappears or improves less than 30 minutes after resuming recumbent position[*]
C. Headache disappears within 14 days of lumbar puncture (if it fails to do so, consider CSF fistula headache)

Cerebrospinal Fluid Fistula Headache
A. Post-traumatic, postoperative, or idiopathic CSF leak demonstrated by measurement of glucose concentration in leaking fluid, or by leakage of spinally injected dye or radioactive tracer
B. Headache has characteristics of postlumbar puncture headache (*vide supra*)
C. Headache disappears within 14 days after effective treatment of fistula [†]

[*] The postural relationship, typically, is much tighter than this, with headache coming on within minutes of getting up and clearing within minutes of lying down. The IHS classification allows for considerable latitude.
[†] Again, typically the CSF fistula headache clears within a day or two of successful repair of the fistula.

Far from being just an academic exercise, a good classification can be a useful diagnostic tool for the clinician. The IHS classification, which is the dominant one, is too long, complex, and unwieldy for easy use by any one other than researchers or headache specialists. In this book, the essence of the diagnostic criteria of the various types of headaches in the IHS classification has been distilled, and incorporated into the clinical descriptions in each chapter.

Bibliography

Headache Classification Committee of The International Headache Society. Classification and diagnostic criteria for headache disorders, cranial neuralgias and facial pain. Cephalalgia 1988; 8 (suppl 7):1–97.

Supplementary Search Strategy

SuSS 1	
Subject	explode Headache (index term)
History	Classification (subheading)
Limited to	Human
AND	1994 through 1997

Chapter 3

PRACTICAL PATHOPHYSIOLOGY OF HEADACHE

Headache, though a common and therefore important condition, is among the most poorly understood of clinical problems. This is largely because until recently we have not had the information that would allow us to think of it in the same analytic way as we do other types of pain, such as chest pain or abdominal pain. Fortunately, the past few decades have brought us new data about headache, which allow us to think about it scientifically. Now we can answer the following questions, which are essential to an understanding of headache:

- What are the pain-sensitive structures that, when stimulated, give rise to headache?
- How are these structures stimulated by disease or dysfunction to generate "pain impulses"?
- How are these impulses modified by the brain to culminate in the varied clinical presentations of headache?

PAIN SENSITIVITY OF THE HEAD

Before advances in anesthesiology made general anesthesia safe for patients with increased intracranial pressure, many neurosurgical procedures were necessarily performed under local anesthesia. From their experience in the 1930s, Ray and Wolff reported pain sensitivity of the head as shown in Table 3.1.

Table 3.1 Pain Sensitive Structures of the Head

Structure	Sensitivity to Pain
Brain parenchyma	Not sensitive
Cranial nerves carrying pain fibers (5,7,9,10)	Sensitive
Arteries of circle of Willis and first few cm of their medium-sized branches	Sensitive
Meningeal (dural) arteries	Sensitive
Large veins in brain and dura	Sensitive
Portions of dura near vessels	Sensitive
Most other parts of dura, arachnoidea, and ependyma	Not sensitive
Structures external to skull: external carotid artery and branches, scalp and neck muscles, skin and cutaneous nerves, cervical nerves and roots, mucosa of sinuses, and teeth	Sensitive

Ray and Wolff mapped out patterns of pain referral in the head that correspond to what we know about the referral of pain in general. Superficial structures refer pain locally. For example, inflammation of the right temporal artery, as in temporal arteritis, produces right temporal headache, and purulent infection of the left frontal sinus causes left forehead pain. Deeper structures refer pain imprecisely, and often to a distant part. For example, sphenoidal sinusitis can cause pain in the vertex, an occipital lobe tumor often produces frontal headache, and irritation of the trigeminal root by a vascular loop in the posterior fossa may result in facial pain. These referral patterns are produced by deep "visceral" pain being interpreted as emanating from the superficial distribution of the involved nerve. Thus, even though an occipital lobe tumor lies well toward the back of the head, it is within the supratentorial cranial compartment, which is innervated by the first division of the trigeminal nerve (V_1); accordingly, the pain is referred to the front half of the head. The posterior fossa (or the infratentorial compartment) is innervated by pain fibers from the second and third cervical nerve roots (C_2 and C_3), which also supply the back of the head. Thus, lesions within the posterior fossa tend to refer pain posteriorly.

Another mechanism of pain referral is "convergence." The caudal nucleus of the trigeminal nerve (Figure 3.1), extending from mid-pons down to the third cervical cord segment. It collects nociceptive impulses not only from the trigeminal nerve but also from the upper cervical segments. Mixing of impulses in this nucleus may cause pain originating in the upper cervical structures to be felt in the front of the head. In this fashion, lesions or dysfunctions in the posterior fossa (innervated by C_2 and C_3) have a mechanism by which they can refer pain to the front of the head. Also, this route may be used by lesions in the upper cervical spine to produce frontal headaches. These "distant referrals" can be confusing for the diagnostician.

In general terms, headache is analogous to the "deep visceral pain" that the clinician grapples with in other parts of the body. The brain is an insensitive organ (at least so far as pain is concerned) surrounded by a pain-sensitive "capsule" consisting of the dura and the surface vessels. Stimulation of this capsule, as with the spleen or liver, produces nonspecific pain that seldom is appreciated precisely at the site of the stimulus, but instead is referred, often widely, through a number of neural pathways and mechanisms. Knowledge of all the possibilities immensely aids diagnosis.

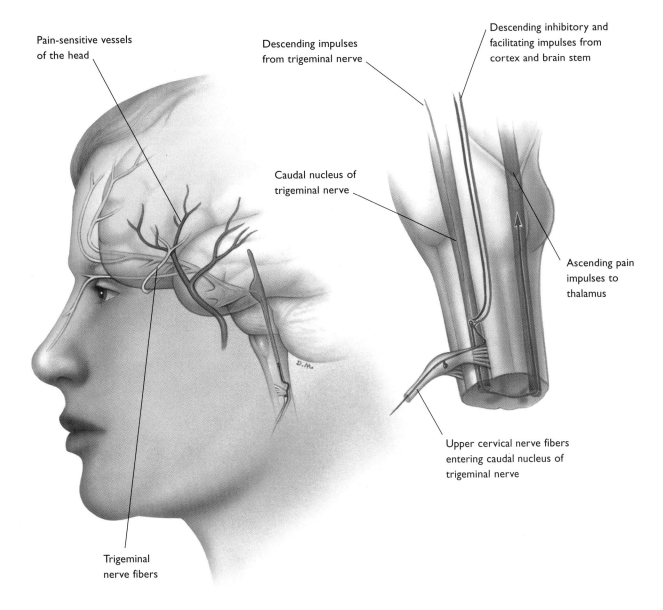

Pain-sensitive vessels of the head

Descending impulses from trigeminal nerve

Descending inhibitory and facilitating impulses from cortex and brain stem

Caudal nucleus of trigeminal nerve

Ascending pain impulses to thalamus

Trigeminal nerve fibers

Upper cervical nerve fibers entering caudal nucleus of trigeminal nerve

Figure 3.1   Pain Innervation of the Head

An important part of the perception of pain is its modification by the central nervous system (CNS). To a large degree, this takes place as the nociceptive impulses enter the CNS, in the caudal nucleus of the trigeminal nerve (see Figure 3.1). Within this structure, these impulses are met by both inhibitory and facilitatory impulses, which descend from higher structures within the cortex and brain stem. Opioid analgesics blunt head pain by activating these descending inhibitory systems, just as anxiety and fear aggravate pain by stimulating the facilitatory systems. Again, these cephalic systems are analogous to those in the dorsal horn of the spinal cord, which modify pain elsewhere in the body. Knowledge of how these systems work allows an opportunity for both pharmacologic and behavioral interventions in the treatment of pain in general and headache in particular.

MECHANISMS OF HEADACHE

When a lesion or disease can be identified as the cause of a headache, the mechanism is usually apparent; where dysfunction is presumed to be the cause, the mechanism is obscure and controversial. Table 3.2 summarizes our present concepts of how and why the various headache syndromes occur.

Table 3.2   How and Why Headache Syndromes Occur

Diseases	Mechanism of Headache Production
Intracranial mass lesions such as brain tumor, hydrocephalus	Displacement (traction) of pain-sensitive vessels
Low intracranial pressure states such as postlumbar puncture headaches	Traction through brain sagging on dural attachments; intracranial vasodilatation
Meningitis, subarachnoid hemorrhage	Inflammation of vessels in meninges and of perivascular dura
Temporal arteritis, intracranial vasculitis	Inflammation of scalp and intracranial vessels
Dysfunctions	
Migraine	Neurally induced dilatation and inflammation of intracranial and extracranial vessels
Cluster headache	Neurally induced inflammation and edema of internal carotid artery
Tension-type headache	Unknown; may be increased sensitivity of pain-mediating systems in brain

MIGRAINE

Recent advances have led to significant improvements in treatment and in our understanding of migraine. The trigeminovascular system is a module that connects the brain to the cranial blood vessels (Figure 3.2). The double-ended trigeminal sensory axon has one terminal on the pain-sensitive cranial vessel and the other in the nucleus trigeminalis of the brain stem. We are all familiar with the afferent function of the trigeminal axon, in which nociceptive impulses from the

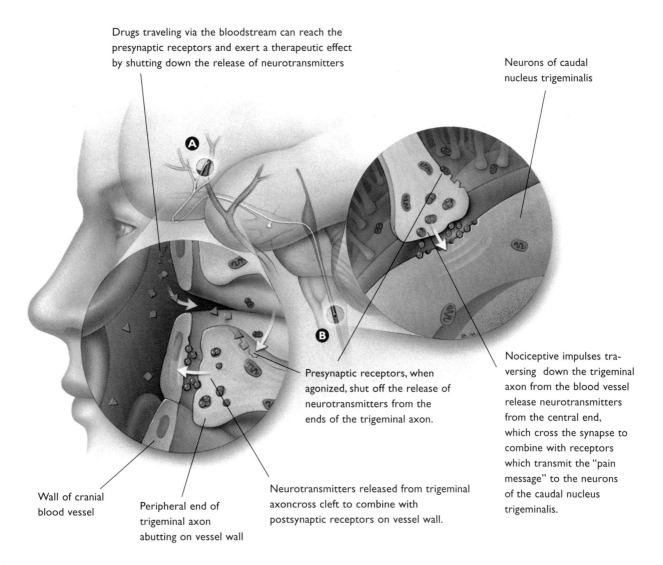

Drugs traveling via the bloodstream can reach the presynaptic receptors and exert a therapeutic effect by shutting down the release of neurotransmitters

Neurons of caudal nucleus trigeminalis

Presynaptic receptors, when agonized, shut off the release of neurotransmitters from the ends of the trigeminal axon.

Nociceptive impulses traversing down the trigeminal axon from the blood vessel release neurotransmitters from the central end, which cross the synapse to combine with receptors which transmit the "pain message" to the neurons of the caudal nucleus trigeminalis.

Wall of cranial blood vessel

Peripheral end of trigeminal axon abutting on vessel wall

Neurotransmitters released from trigeminal axoncross cleft to combine with postsynaptic receptors on vessel wall.

Figure 3.2   The trigeminal nerve has one foot (A) on the blood vessels, and the other foot (B) in the caudal nucleus trigeminalis in the brain stem.

blood vessels (Figure 3.3) and other pain-sensitive intracranial structures (Figure 3.4) are transmitted orthodromically (i.e., in the "usual" direction) to reach the caudal nucleus of the trigeminal nerve in the CNS, to "register" as pain. Less well appreciated is that the trigeminal "sensory" axon can be traversed in the opposite direction (antidromic transmission), providing a route by which impulses descending from cortical and other higher centers in the CNS can reach the blood vessels of the head. Once at the distal end of the trigeminal axon, in the immediate vicinity

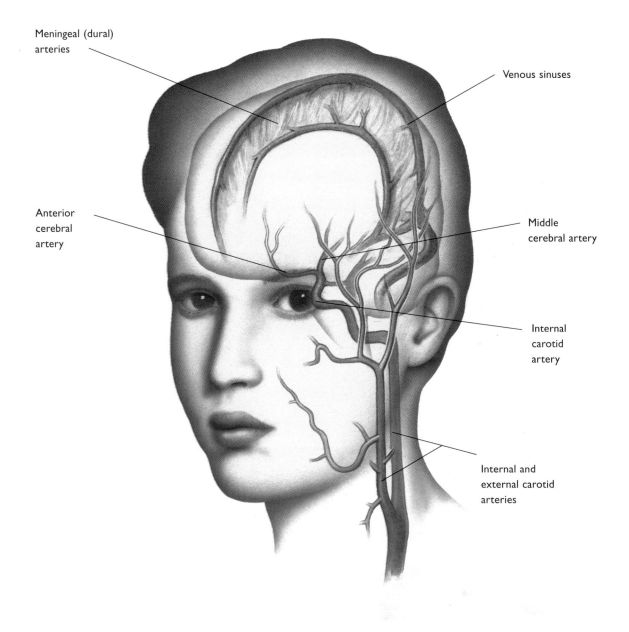

Meningeal (dural) arteries

Venous sinuses

Anterior cerebral artery

Middle cerebral artery

Internal carotid artery

Internal and external carotid arteries

Figure 3.3   Vascular Pain Sensitive Structures

of the blood vessel, these impulses cause the secretion from the distal axon terminal of neurotransmitters such as substance P and calcium gene-related peptide (CGRP). These transmitters combine with receptors in the vessel wall to produce inflammation and dilatation (neurogenic inflammation) of the vessel. The distressed vessel then sends pain impulses back up the axon to the brain stem, thence to the thalamus and cortex, where the pain is "registered" as a throbbing headache.

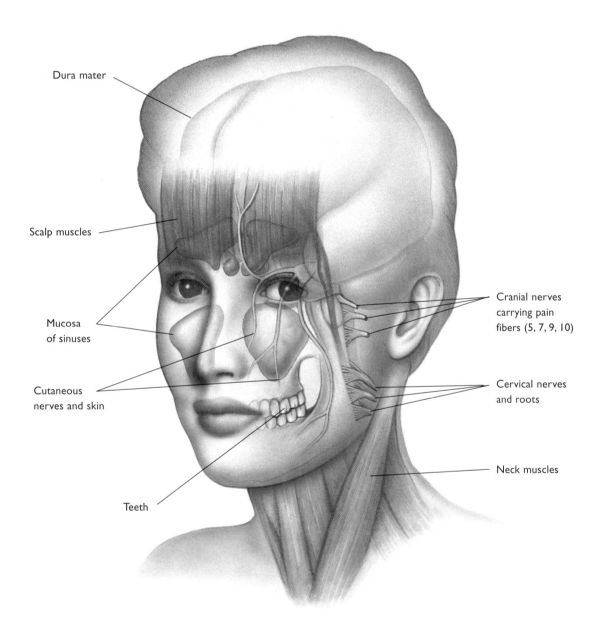

Figure 3.4   Nonvascular Pain-Sensitive Structures

A migraine attack, viewed according to this model, is "neurovascular ping-pong," with influences descending to the trigeminal apparatus from higher centers causing it to produce neurogenic inflammation in the cranial blood vessels, which in turn send pain impulses back up to the brain to produce the headache. Exactly how the central (or CNS) end of the trigeminal axon is stimulated by the brain to set the migraine cascade in motion remains a bit of a mystery, but electrical events within the cerebral cortex (spreading depression) have been implicated. Other central mechanisms may include innate (possibly genetically determined) biochemical dysfunction. For example, magnetic resonance spectroscopy studies have shown decreased intracellular magnesium levels in the brains of migraine sufferers both during and between attacks, which could trigger spreading depression. With the demonstration that some kinships of familial hemiplegic migraine share a gene anomaly on chromosome 19, there has been renewed interest in the genetics of migraine, with hopes of establishing the "core" metabolic defect in migraine and of finding a diagnostic migraine "marker."

It is important to note that an older concept of migraine pathophysiology, that vasoconstriction and ischemia of the cerebral cortex are responsible for the migraine aura and in some way for generating the migraine attack, has been abandoned by most authorities for lack of supporting evidence. Most of the available data point to migraine being a primary neurologic event, which sets in motion a cascade of phenomena, one of which is "neurogenic inflammation" of cranial blood vessels.

The modern concepts of the trigeminovascular system and neurogenic inflammation have permitted understanding of how some established migraine drugs work, such as ergotamine and dihydroergotamine. They have also generated new treatments such as sumatriptan and related medications. At both ends of the trigeminal axon there are presynaptic receptors, styled 5-HT_{1D} receptors, which when activated by the naturally occurring neurotransmitter, serotonin, shut off the flow of neurotransmitters such as substance P and CGRP from the ends of the axon. This in turn shuts down the mechanism of neurogenic inflammation at the vascular end of the axon, and the mechanism of pain transmission at the CNS end (see Figure 3.2). Ergotamine, dihydroergotamine, sumatriptan and the many sumatriptan-like drugs under development all combine with varying degrees of selectivity with the 5-HT_{1D} receptors to activate them and thus to reduce the release of some of the neurotransmitters from the trigeminal axons.

TENSION-TYPE HEADACHE

Although tension-type headaches are at least three times as common as migraine, we know far less about them. The great European clinicians of the nineteenth century recognized that while some headaches were due to discernible lesions, and many were due to migraine, there remained a vast motley of headaches of no apparent cause. Some of these clinicians, like Romberg and Gowers, considered these headaches to be psychological. Osler, on the other hand, thought that they were due to muscle pain, possibly rheumatic in origin. Wolff's group, in the 1940s, united the psychological and physical by proposing that these common headaches, then known as "tension headaches," were due to stress-induced involuntary contraction of the muscles of the scalp and neck. Initially accepted with enthusiasm, this concept of "muscle contraction headaches" has now been invalidated by numerous observations that these headaches can occur in the total absence of any muscle contraction. It may be that they arise more centrally, from "irritability" of the caudal nucleus of the trigeminal nerve and other CNS structures that register, modulate, and interpret head pain. We simply do not know. The current term, "tension-type headaches," because purposefully vague and uninformative, is accurate.

Some authors have even expressed doubt whether tension-type headaches exist as an entity separate and distinct from migraine. Others believe that it is possible to distinguish between them with a sufficiently careful history. We share this belief. Certainly, treatments effective for migraine are largely useless in tension-type headaches, an observation favoring their mutual distinctiveness.

Tension-type headaches are one of the least investigated areas of headache. Learning more about how and why they occur is essential if we are to find an effective treatment for this common and debilitating entity.

Bibliography

Basbaum AI, Fields HL. Endogenous pain control systems: brainstem spinal pathways and endorphin circuitry. Ann Rev Neurosci 1984; 7:309–338.

Edmeads J. Headache and facial pain. In: Stein JH, ed. Internal medicine. 4th ed. St. Louis: Mosby, 1994:1025–1033.

Goadsby PJ, Edvinnson L. The trigeminovascular system and migraine: studies characterizing cerebrovascular and neuropeptide changes seen in humans and cats. Ann Neurol 1993; 33:48–56.

Joutel A, Bousser MG, Bioussee V, et al. A gene for familial hemiplegic migraine maps to chromosome 19. Nature Genetics 1993; 5:40–45.

Moskowitz MA. Neurogenic inflammation in the pathophysiology and treatment of migraine. Neurology 1993; 43(Suppl 3):S16–S20.

Moskowitz MA, Nozaki K, Kraig RP. Neocortical spreading depression provokes the expression of c-fos protein-like immunoreactivity within trigeminal nucleus caudalis via trigemino-vascular mechanisms. J Neurosci 1993; 13:1167–1177.

Raskin NH. Headache. 2nd ed. New York: Churchill Livingstone, 1988:221.

Rasmussen BK, Jensen J, Olesen J. A population-based analysis of the diagnostic criteria of the International Headache Society. Cephalalgia 1991; 11:129–134.

Ray BS, Wolff HG. Experimental studies on headache: pain sensitive structures of the head and their significance in headache. Arch Surg 1940; 41:813–856.

Schoenen J. Exteroceptive suppression of temporalis muscle activity in patients with chronic headaches and normal volunteers. Methodology, clinical and pathophysiological relevance. Headache 1993; 33:317–322.

Simons DJ, Day E, Goodell H, Wolff HG. Experimental studies on headache: muscles of the scalp and neck as sources of pain. Assoc Res Nerv Ment Dis 1943; 23:228–241.

Welch KMA, Barkley GL, Tepley N, Ramadan NM. Central neurogenic mechanisms of migraine. Neurology 1993; 43(Suppl 3):S21–S25.

Zwart JA, Bovim G, Sand T, Sjaastad O. Tension headache: botulinum toxin in paralysis of temporal muscles. Headache 1994; 34:458–462.

Supplementary Search Strategy

SuSS I	
Subject	Tension Headache (major index term)
Subject	Physiopathology (subheading)
Limited to	Human
AND	1994 through 1997

Chapter 4

HISTORY AND PHYSICAL EXAMINATION

HISTORY TAKING

Headache is among the most common complaints presenting to a family physician.
The usual paucity of physical findings makes history the "gold standard" in its
diagnosis. A systematic approach that includes description of the headache, its
temporal profile, relieving and exacerbating factors, medications, and general
health status will assist the clinician in distinguishing "benign" from more sinister
causes of headache. Appended to this chapter is a history-taking questionnaire to
facilitate the process and help assure comprehensiveness. Often the same patient
may exhibit more than one type of headache. The clinician should attempt to
clarify each of these.

Temporal Profile

The mode of onset of the headache and its behavior over time are the first critical
points. A *chronic* cyclic/recurrent or *longstanding* daily headache usually represents
a primary disorder such as migraine, cluster, or tension-type headache.
Progressively worsening headaches (weeks to months) suggest increasing intracranial pressure or systemic disease. While focal lateralizing neurologic symptoms will
raise immediate concern, patients with benign intracranial hypertension, bilateral
subdural hematomas, midline obstructive lesions, and chronic meningitic syndromes may exhibit *only* a subacute or progressive headache.

Abrupt onset headaches suggest a vascular mechanism such as subarachnoid
hemmorhage. Some infections and ophthalmic headache syndromes may also begin
suddenly. Usually, "tell-tale" features on physical examination will distinguish
between these serious conditions.

Other headaches, despite their cataclysmic onset, have a benign prognosis. Coital, cough, exertional, thunderclap, and "crash" or "blitz" migraine headaches can only be diagnosed in retrospect after their cyclical nature becomes manifest and after investigations provide no evidence of a lesion.

The rapid onset pain associated with cluster headaches, SUNCT (short unilateral neuralgic pain with conjunctival injection and tearing) syndrome, and trigeminal neuralgia, rarely poses a diagnostic quandary as the characteristics of each of these are distinctive. Finally, ice-pick headaches ("jabs and jolts") are fleeting, often multifocal cranial pains which, despite their intensity, are invariably benign.

Location and Character of Headache

The location of pain can be an important clue to the etiology. Burning or pulsating ocular or peri-retroorbital pain ("salt and pepper in the face/eye"), may reflect incipient ischemia in the vertebrobasilar territory, an expanding skull-base aneurysm, cluster headache, SUNCT syndrome, extracranial or intracranial vascular dissection, dural sinus occlusion, or inflammation in the cavernous sinus. Nonvascular causes include ophthalmic and inflammatory meningeal syndromes. Infratentorial, occipitonuchal, and cervical spine pathology can also refer pain to the forehead or eye because of the convergence of C2-3 nociceptive afferents with trigeminal afferents in the caudal trigeminal nucleus in the brainstem.

Unilateral pulsatile or throbbing headaches usually indicate a vascular mechanism, most notably migraine. The headache location in a migraineur, however, fluctuates over the course of an attack and between different attacks. Occipitonuchal and bifrontal/temporal pain is also characteristic of migraine, with the pain sometimes having started or remaining maximal on one side. Chronic holocephalic or band-like pressure is characteristic of tension-type headache; rarely, it can be symptomatic of an underlying mass causing increased intracranial pressure.

As blood or pus tracks down the subarachnoid space, the acute headache of a subarachnoid hemorrhage or meningitis may be followed by pain that travels down the spinal column into the interscapular region or low back. This sequence should always alert the clinician to suspect meningeal irritation.

Symptoms Associated With Headache

Headache-associated symptoms can be helpful in assessing baleful headaches. Nausea, vomiting, photo- and phonophobia are characteristic of migraine but, in the absence of a known history of migraine, should prompt consideration of an infectious or space-occupying lesion in the head, or of a systemic illness.

Premonitory Symptoms

Antecedent transient visual symptoms support a diagnosis of migraine; however, progressive impairment of visual acuity with transient visual obscurations (with or without disc-related visual field cuts or papilledema), may be seen in patients with headaches caused by raised intracranial pressure. Amaurosis may be seen in patients with anterior ischemic optic neuropathy secondary to vasculitis (e.g., giant cell arteritis), or retinal emboli from an atherosclerotic or dissecting carotid artery. Diplopia with head pain may signify a parasellar mass, a posterior communicating artery aneurysm, or the Tolosa-Hunt syndrome.

A sensory "march" (traveling paresthesias) evolving over 15 to 20 minutes is typical of migraine; however, first attacks of these relatively rare varieties of migraine may mandate further neurologic investigations. Cheiro-oral migraine with traveling hand and face paresthesias can mimic partial sensory seizures, transient ischemic attack (TIA), or an underlying vascular anomaly (e.g., arteriovenous malformation). Hemiplegic, ophthalmoplegic, basilar, and confusional migraine often present with such obvious and frightening neurologic symptoms (and signs) that their ominous mimics rarely escape detection.

Precipitating Factors

Although exertion, cough, sneeze, strain, coitus, sudden head turning, and bending may be associated with benign headache syndromes, this can usually only be determined after a negative search for subarachnoid hemorrhage or "sentinel" headache (coital and exertional headaches), and midline obstructive lesions (colloid cyst of the third ventricle and Arnold-Chiari malformation).

When the headaches are associated with menses, ovulation, stress, dietary triggers, hormonal supplements, fatigue, depression, and sleep or food deprivation, migraine is likely.

Headaches aggravated by upright posture suggest intracranial hypotension, which can occur spontaneously or iatrogenically. The supine position, or a change in position, may worsen the headaches of intracranial hypertension.

Family History

In the appropriate clinical context, a family history replete with migraine, particularly of the less common variants (basilar, hemiplegic), supports this diagnosis. A family history of intracranial saccular aneurysms, polycystic kidney disease, or brain tumors should prompt additional investigations.

Medical History

The general medical history and a careful review of systems are essential in history-taking. An underlying history of carcinoma should prompt the clinician to consider the possibility of a metastatic lesion, especially breast cancer, melanoma, renal cell carcinoma, and lung cancer. A history of vascular headaches in an individual with repeated spontaneous abortions or thromboembolic events may suggest an associated antiphospholipid syndrome. Head trauma may predispose the patient to post-traumatic headaches or possibly an underlying subdural hematoma or extracranial arterial dissection. A wide variety of disorders associated with dental, sinuse, or ear, nose, and throat abnormalities may present as headache. Chronic daily headache can frequently be the initial complaint in depression.

The social history should review environmental factors such as a major change in lifestyle and potential areas of stress that could be contributing to the headache. A change in sleep habits, as in cases of sleep apnea where early morning headaches may occur, should be explored.

In the review of systems, a careful history of allergic reactions should be elicited so that the clinician can select appropriate medical therapy. Systems review is also a necessary part of the decision-making process in medical management. Conditions such as diabetes and asthma, for example, would contraindicate use of beta-blocker therapy in migraine headaches.

"RED FLAGS"

After eliciting a detailed history, the following headache-associated features should always cause concern and warrant immediate referral and investigation:

- Abrupt onset or an unusually severe headache, particularly if associated with neurologic symptoms. A complaint that a particular headache is "different" than others previously experienced, should always be pursued.
- Subacute or progressive headache over days to months.
- Headache associated with nausea, vomiting, and fever not explained by systemic illness, such as the "flu."
- New onset headache in adult life (>40 years), or a significant change of a long-standing headache problem.
- Precipitation of headache by Valsalva (cough, sneeze, strain), position change, head turning, exercise, or coitus.
- Headaches associated with nocturnal occurrence or morning awakening.

- Headaches associated with neurologic signs or symptoms such as confusion, decreased level of alertness or consciousness or cognition, meningismus, or papilledema.
- Systemic symptoms such as fever, jaw claudication, weight loss, myalgia.

PHYSICAL EXAMINATION

Although a detailed neurologic examination is part of the clinical evaluation of headache, certain aspects of the general examination should also be included.

Routine vital signs are an essential component of any examination and, in cases of headache, can help to exclude causes such as severe hypertension, meningitis, or systemic febrile illnesses. Auscultation of bruits over carotid and vertebral arteries and the orbit can alert the clinician to potential arterial stenosis or dissection, and arteriovenous malformations. Trigger point areas of tenderness, masses, skull defects, hematomas, and bruises are detected by simple palpation of head and neck. Temporal mandibular joint problems may at times be associated with headache and should be considered if there is tenderness or limitations of movement of the temporal mandibular joint. Palpation of the superficial temporal arteries can reveal thickened, enlarged vessels with diminished pulse, associated in some cases with tender red scalp nodules in patients with temporal arteritis. The diagnosis is supported by an elevated erythrocyte sedimentation rate and confirmed with a temporal artery biopsy.

During cluster headache attacks, patients may present with lacrimation and rhinorrhea, facial flushing, ptosis, and miosis (partial Horner's syndrome). Some patients with cluster headaches have "leonine facies" with thickened, heavy creased skin and coarse features (see Figure 9.1).

A Horner's syndrome accompanied by lacrimation and conjunctival injection is characteristic of cluster headache, but a painful Horner's syndrome in the absence of a cluster history may signify a carotid artery dissection.

Diffuse skin changes may suggest a variety of etiologies for headache. For example, café au lait spots may suggest neurofibromatosis which is associated with intracranial meningiomas and schwannomas. Dry skin, alopecia, and swelling are seen with hypothyroidism. The clinician should be aware of occult malignant melanotic lesions that may be detected on the skin and be associated with potentially metastatic disease to the brain.

Trigger point tenderness around the cervical spine associated with muscle spasm and diminished range of motion may suggest a "cervicogenic" cause for the headache. Nuchal rigidity due to meningeal irritation, seen with subarachnoid hemorrhage and meningitis, needs prompt workup and referral.

The mental status of the patient may be assessed during the history taking. It is important to determine the patient's affect, his or her ability to concentrate and recall details of past history, and whether there are accompanying difficulties in comprehension or with speech. If difficulties are suspected while taking the history, a detailed mental status examination should be pursued.

Cranial nerve examination may yield clues regarding the etiology of the headache. While disruption of smell is most often due to incidental nasal pathology or to remote head trauma, it may reflect symptoms of olfactory groove or fronto-temporal tumors.

The fundoscopic examination is an essential part of the workup of the headache patient. Evidence of hemorrhage or papilledema (Figure 4.1) warrants prompt imaging to rule out a space occupying lesion. If a screening visual field examination is abnormal, a formal field assessment should be performed to help localize a lesion (e.g., pituitary tumor, which may have associated bitemporal visual field defects). Ocular movement abnormalities suggest raised intrcranial pressure or secondary involvement of oculomotor nerves.

Palpation of the scalp, face, and tapping of teeth may trigger pain as in trigeminal neuralgia, or suggest local pathology in these structures.

Facial symmetry may be observed with the patient at rest. Minor asymmetries may become more obvious with voluntary activation of muscle groups (e.g., frowning, smiling, blowing, puffing cheeks, and raising eyebrows). Upper

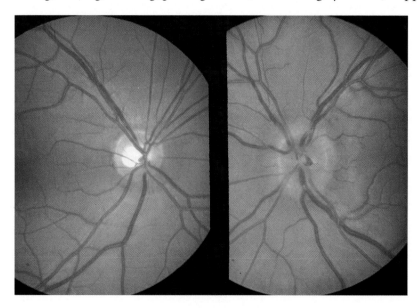

Figure 4.1   Papilledema seen on fundoscopic examination. Note the normal disc (left) as compared to the papilledema seen on the right.

motor neuron facial weakness may be differentiated from lower motor neuron involvement on the basis of frontalis muscle involvement in the latter.

Cranial nerves supplying the tongue, gag-reflex, and bulbar muscles can be affected by a wide variety of causes. If the involvement is patchy, asymmetric, and progressive, infiltrative causes such as neoplasm, tuberculous meningitis, and sarcoid can be investigated best with MRI and lumbar puncture.

The motor examination can be divided into categories of bulk, power, tone, involuntary movements, and gait. Lesions of the brain and spinal cord manifest themselves with increased tone, weakness and hyperreflexia, while weakness, atrophy, presence of fasciculations, and diminished tendon reflexes suggest a lesion at the root, plexus or peripheral nerve level. Evidence of truncal instability suggests a midline cerebellar lesion, whereas limb incoordination (e.g., heel-to-shin or finger-to-nose dysmetria) are indicative of ipsilateral cerebellar hemispheric lesions.

As with motor function, sensory abnormalities can be associated with central and peripheral lesions. Astereognosis, (failure to recognize shape and size of objects) and graphesthesia (failure to recognize a letter or number drawn on the patient's hand), are typical of parietal sensory dysfunctions. Midline sensory defects usually reflect a central etiology.

In assessing deep tendon reflexes, the presence of reflex asymmetry between opposite limbs is clinically significant, but it must be assessed in the context of other findings. The presence of unilateral hyperreflexia with an upgoing toe is indicative of a pyramidal lesion.

Although the neurologic examination in the headache patient is in most cases normal, its importance to clinician and patient cannot be underestimated. The presence of focal deficits on examination or evidence of "red flags" on history should prompt the physician to undertake further workup.

Bibliography

Dalessio DJ. Diagnosing the severe headache. Neurology 1994; 44(Suppl 3):S6–S12.

Diamond S, Dalessio DJ. Taking a headache history. In: Diamond S, Dalessio DJ. The practicing Physician's Approach. 5th ed. Baltimore: Williams & Wilkins, 1992:25–30.

Diamond S, Dalessio DJ. Taking a headache history. In: Tollison CD, Kunkel RS, eds. Headache diagnosis and treatment. 5th ed. Baltimore: Williams & Wilkins, 1993:11–24.

Newman LC, Lipton RB, Solomon S. Headache history and neurological examination. In: Tollison CD, Kunkel RS, eds. Headache diagnosis and treatment. 1st ed. Baltimore: Williams & Wilkins, 1993:23–30.

Critical Decisions

A

- Abrupt onset headache may suggest vascular or hemorrhagic cause—to be ruled out.
- New onset headache or a change from usual headache pattern warrants further investigation.

B Danger signals

- Abrupt onset severe headache or change in usual pattern.
- Associated nausea, vomiting, or fever
- New onset over age 40.
- Worsening headache with straining.
- Nocturnal headache.
- Associated confusion, delirium, loss of consciousness, nuchal rigidity, or papilledema.
- Associated systemic symptoms, including fever, weight loss, myalgia, or jaw claudication.

C Medication history

- Careful attention should be paid to OTC medication taken—the amount, frequency, and effectiveness.
- Include a history of previous migraine treatments used and the results.

D

- Progressive visual symptoms of impairment, visual field cut and transient visual obscurations may be seen with raised intracranial pressure.
- Examine for papilledema, visual field deficit, pupil abnormalities, extraocular movement, palsies.

E

- Beware of *painful* Horner's syndrome in the absence of cluster history, suggesting possible carotid artery dissection.
- Examine for carotid/vertebral bruits and focal neurologic signs.

F

- Exertional headaches also associated with subarachnoid hemorrhage and intracranial mass lesions.
- Examine for nuchal rigidity, papilledema, any focal neurologic findings.

Headache Diagnosis

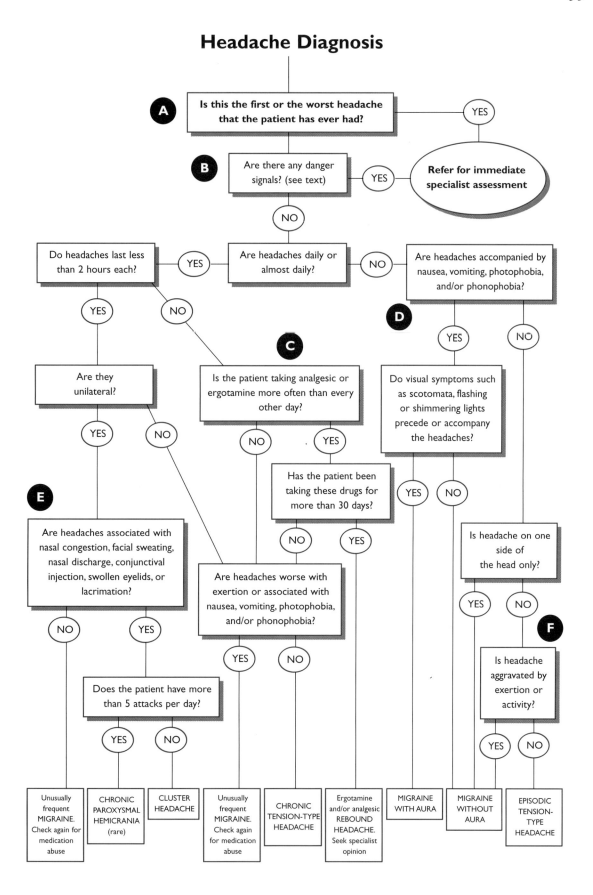

Supplementary Search Strategy

SuSS I

Subject	explode Headache (index term)
Subject	explode Medical History Taking (index term) or explode Physical Examination (index term)
Limited to	Human
AND	1994 through 1997

APPENDIX 1: HISTORY-TAKING QUESTIONNAIRE FOR THE HEADACHE PATIENT

- Has there been a recent change or escalation in the onset, frequency, duration, or usual pattern of your headache?
- Do you know if there are any factors that trigger your headache? (e.g., food, weather, menses, alcohol)
- Is there an aura associated with your headache?
- Has the severity of your headache increased?
- Where is the pain located? Is it consistently on the same side?
- Is your headache pain throbbing, aching or stabbing?
- Is your headache aggravated by exertion such as coughing, sneezing, exercising, or bending?
- Do you experience nausea or vomiting with your headache?
- Do you have other symptoms such as extreme sensitivity to light or sound, loss of vision, fever, or sensory changes?
- What treatment are you receiving for your headache at present? What have you tried in the past?
- Have you had x-ray or lab work done for your headache in the past?
- Have you experienced any recent change in lifestyle, particularly in your sleep habits or work stress?
- Does anyone else in your family suffer from headaches regularly?
- What medications—prescription or OTC—are you taking at present, for headache or any other problem?
- What other medical problems have you had that have been treated with medicines or required surgery?
- Do you have any known allergies?
- Do you smoke? How much? Do you drink alcohol? How much? Do you take recreational drugs? (what and how much)

Chapter 5

RADIOLOGIC INVESTIGATION OF HEADACHE

Headache is the most common complaint made by patients to their family physicians. The majority represent benign dysfunctional headache syndromes (migraine, tension-type headache). However, because headache may be a symptom of a wider variety of disease, recognizing which cases require investigation beyond the history and physical examination continues to challenge the practicing physician.

Certain features of the history warrant further investigation. These include sudden onset headache in the absence of a preceding history of headache; new associated neurologic symptoms such as visual change, nocturnal awakening with headache, or associated nausea and vomiting; and precipitation of headache by exertion or strain, suggesting increased intracranial pressure. In a patient with a past history of common migraine now presenting with associated neurologic symptoms, further investigations would be advised. Any new onset headache in the elderly must be investigated and considered to be secondary to organic disease until proven otherwise. Also, associated symptoms including nuchal rigidity, fever, focal neurologic signs, or deficits, should prompt the physician to search for an underlying cause.

In the past, noninvasive investigation of headache consisted solely of skull radiographs which, although low in cost, provided limited information. Invasive procedures such as pneumoencephalography and cerebral angiography, were reserved for those in whom more sinister lesions were suspected. The introduction of computerized tomography (CT) and magnetic resonance imaging (MRI) has revolutionized neuroradiologic diagnosis. Although MRI is superior to CT in its sensitivity, CT scanning remains an important evaluation tool.

Cerebral angiography is useful in the diagnosis of headache where vascular abnormalities such as aneurysm, arteriovenous malformation, and occlusive vascular disease are suspected; however, since it is invasive, the use of angiography should be limited to these situations.

Often, the primary purpose of radiologic investigation of headache is to exclude the possibility of lesions.

Critical Decisions

A Suspect lesion
- Posterior fossa, brain stem, and pituitary lesions may not be well-visualized on CT unless they are large (> 2 cm diameter).
- MRI is the procedure of choice in visualizing these areas.

B Suspect bleed, hematoma, tumor, or infarct
- CT can be performed with or without contrast.
- More vascular lesions (e.g., tumors, AVM) may be visualized more clearly with contrast; however, in cases where recent bleeding is suspected, CT without contrast is recommended.

C Suspect aneurysm or AVM
- 3-D CT angiography visualizes intracranial vascular abnormalities.
- Advantages: rapid accessibility, reduced examination time, and ease of use in the intubated patients.
- A useful, less invasive screening tool in the asymptomatic patient at higher risk of cerebral aneurysm.

D CT positive, infarct suspected
- Investigate underlying source in cases of cerebral infarct confirmed on CT.
- Carotid doppler may identify significant stenosis or evidence of underlying plaque as source of embolism.
- Echocardiography and Holter monitor will determine cardiac source of embolism.

E CT negative, symptoms persist
- Cerebral angiography remains investigation of choice in vascular lesions.

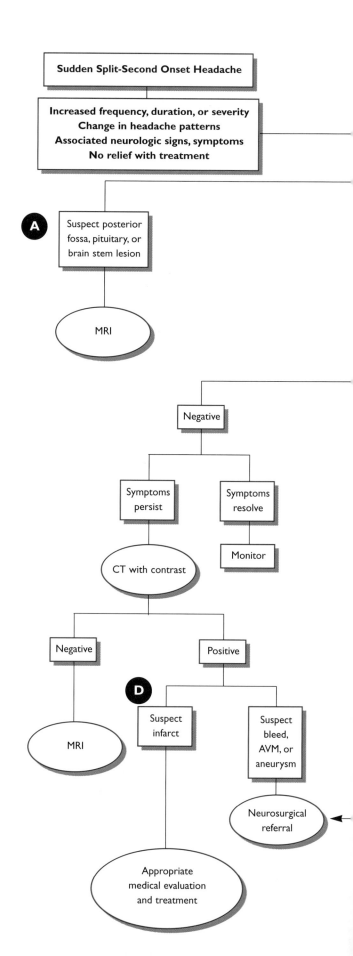

Radiologic Assessment of Headache

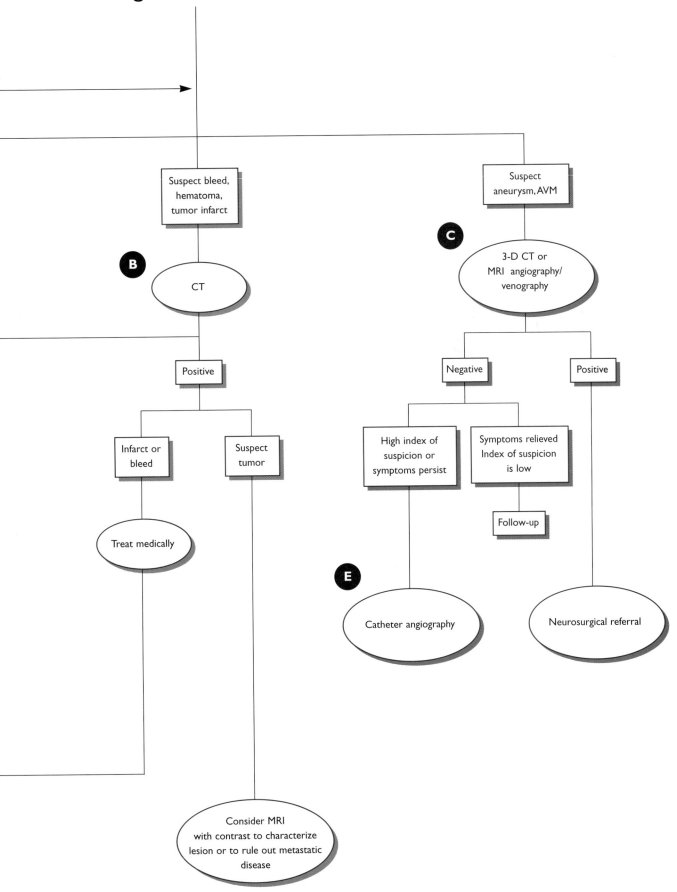

COMPUTERIZED TOMOGRAPHY

In headache of abrupt or recent onset, with escalation in frequency and severity of symptoms or with associated neurologic signs or symptoms, CT scanning should be considered. Headache may be the first sign of a wide variety of intracranial lesions, including tumor, aneurysm, arteriovenous malformation, or hemorrhage. Where tumor is suspected, the accuracy of detection using CT scanning is greater than 90% when intravenous contrast is used. CT scan is the preferred imaging modality to exclude the possibility of intracranial pathology in patients with headache.

CT scanning can be performed with or without contrast. The contrast agent, which is given intravenously, crosses the disrupted blood-brain barrier. Therefore more vascular lesions such as tumors may be more clearly visualized with the use of contrast. When intracranial or subarachnoid hemorrhage is suspected, CT scan without contrast is recommended because of its ability to detect recent bleeds. Although localized intracranial hematomas are easily detected, small subarachnoid hemorrhages may not be identified as readily and further investigation using lumbar puncture may be required. In patients whose clinical presentation consists of sudden onset of severe headache with associated neck stiffness and/or focal neurologic signs, and in whom subarachnoid hemorrhage is suspected, a lumbar puncture is warranted even if the results of the CT scan are normal.

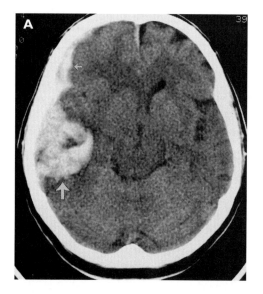 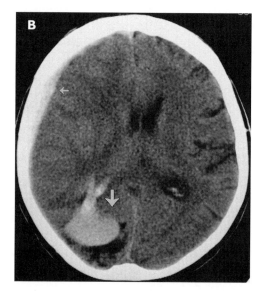

Figure 5.1 Patient with sudden onset severe headache and progressive loss of consciousness. *A,* CT scan without contrast, demonstrating an area of high attenuation (arrow) in the right temporal lobe, consistent with intraparenchymal bleeding. There is also a crescent-shaped area of high attenuation adjacent to the frontal cortex representing an acute subdural hematoma. *B,* Scans at a higher level show the subdural hematoma (small arrow) and blood in the dilated occipital horn of the right lateral ventricle (large arrow).

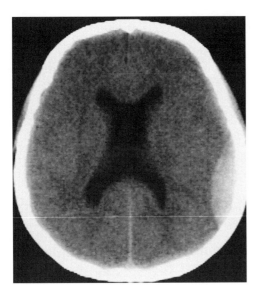

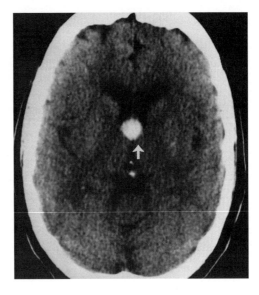

Figure 5.2 CT scan of a 70-year-old male with increasing headache. The scan demonstrates a lenticular area of increased attenuation, consistent with an epidural hematoma. Compare the lens shape of an epidural hematoma to the crescent shape of a subdural hematoma that conforms to the surface of the brain (Figure 5.1).

Figure 5.3 CT scan with contrast of a patient with left temporal headache. A colloid cyst of the third ventricle (a round area of high attenuation) is visible in the midline (arrow).

CT scan with contrast can also detect large aneurysms; however, those less than 2 cm in diameter may not be discernible without MRI or angiography.

Although angiography is the investigation of choice for assessment of the cerebral vasculature, as an invasive procedure it carries with it the risk of such complications as hemorrhage from the puncture site, vasospasm, and stroke. Because delays occur when arranging for an angiogram, it may be less than an ideal choice for assessing acute subarachnoid hemorrhage. The advent of helical CT has made it possible to visualize intracranial vascular abnormalities with the use of CT angiography. The advantages of CT angiography over MR angiography include more rapid accessibility along with reduced examination time (less than 30 minutes), and its facility with intubated patients or patients with magnetic vascular clips. Similarly, three-dimensional CT angiography is less expensive and less invasive than conventional angiography. It is a useful screening tool in the asymptomatic patient who may be at higher risk of cerebral aneurysm (e.g., positive family history).

Acute intracranial bleeding can be identified on a CT scan as an area of increased density. In time, however, the appearance of the bleed will change with clot lysis and may eventually become equal in density to the surrounding brain tissue.

In patients with headache caused by acute obstructive hydrocephalus, CT scans or MRI may be able to differentiate neoplasms, benign cysts, or meningiomas. In this situation the headache may be positional and may be exacerbated when the patient lies down.

In chronic headache where there is an absence of neurologic signs, studies suggest that there is less than a 1% incidence of abnormal CT findings. Although CT scans in migraine are usually normal, associated atrophy, ischemic changes, and cerebral edema have been reported in a few series. Complicated migraine with associated neurologic deficits may be identified by an area of infarction on CT scan. No significant correlation exists between severity, location of headache, complicating factors, age, time of onset of attack, hypertension, nausea or vomiting, handedness, and any CT measurements. The etiology and significance of these changes remains unknown.

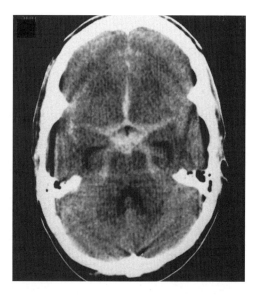

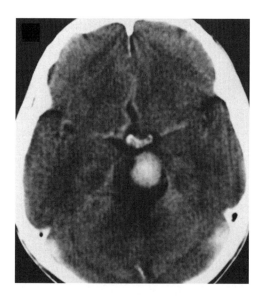

Figure 5.4 CT scan of a 25-year-old female who reported sudden onset of exertional headache. Instead of the usual dark appearance of the suprasellar and parasellar cisterns, the cisterns are white, consistent with acute subarachnoid bleeding.

Figure 5.5 CT scan with contrast of a 37-year-old male who complained of a headache of gradual onset and whose pupils were dilated. The scan reveals a 2-cm enhancing lesion in the region of the posterior cerebral artery, consistent with an aneurysm.

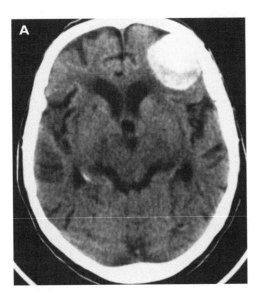 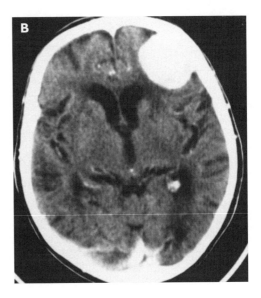

Figure 5.6   CT scans of a 50-year-old male who exhibited slowly progressive right-sided weakness and bilateral headaches. *A*, CT without contrast reveals calcified mass in the left front lobe. *B*, CT scan with contrast shows homogeneous enhancement of the noncalcified portion of the tumor. The pre- and post-contrast appearance of the tumor is consistent with a meningioma.

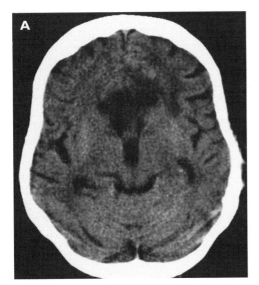 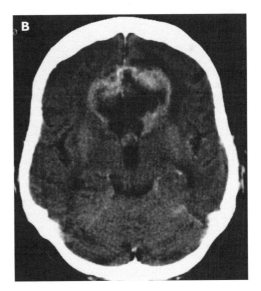

Figure 5.7   CT scans of a 42-year-old female who presented with gradually increasing headache, personality change, and right-sided weakness. *A*, Precontrast CT identifies an area of low attenuation in the midline anterior to the ventricles involving the corpus callosum. *B*, Contrast CT scan shows ring enhancement of a "butterfly" high-grade glioma.

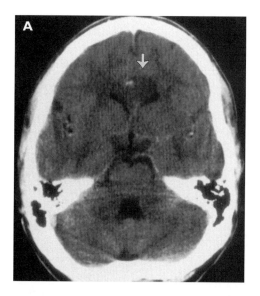

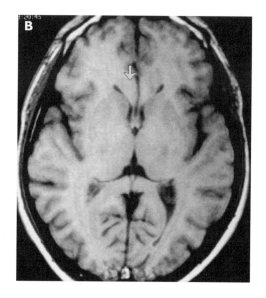

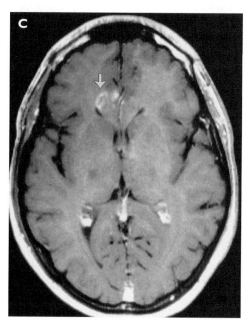

Figure 5.8   CT and MR scans of a 60-year-old asymptomatic woman with a history of breast cancer. *A,* CT scan with contrast demonstrates a subtle area of decreased attenuation in the corpus callosum. *B,* T₁ weighted MRI again demonstrating a subtle area of abnormality within the corpus callosum. *C,* MRI with IV gadolinium demonstrating an obvious area of enhancement consistent with tumor. Note: This lesion, being quite small, is unlikely to cause headache at this stage.

MAGNETIC RESONANCE IMAGING

MRI possesses greater sensitivity than CT in detecting brain pathology. The high resolution of the image, the improved delineation of the lesion, the multiplanar views available, and the absence of bone artifact make MRI the superior imaging procedure. However, the presence of magnetic clips or pacemakers can impair its usefulness. The patient's weight (if in excess of 250 lb), and claustrophobia may also be limiting factors.

With the use of gadolinium, an intravenous contrast agent, sensitivity in tumor detection is further improved. MRI with gadolinium is the imaging technique of choice to demonstrate meningeal pathology. This agent localizes to hyperemic tissue by passing through the blood-brain barrier, particularly in the case of dural and meningeal inflammation. Thus it is particularly valuable in the diagnosis of meningitis and encephalitis.

Herpes encephalitis is often detected by MRI within the first one or two days of onset. Similarly, other infections, vasculitis, and intracranial abscesses can now be detected earlier with the use of MRI and gadolinium.

Although a CT scan detects most brain tumors, MRI may detect small tumors of only a few millimeters in diameter and infiltrating tumors that may be missed on a CT scan.

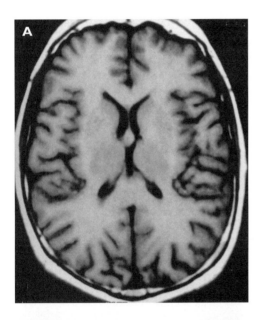

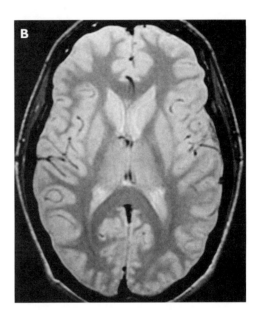

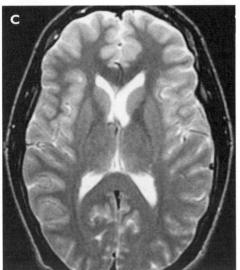

Figure 5.9 MR images of normal brain A, T₁ weighted axial image with cerebrospinal fluid (CSF) appearing black. Gray matter appears gray, and white matter white. B, Proton density MRI. CSF and gray matter appear similar and white matter is darker. C, T₂ weighted axial image. CSF is white and white matter appears dark gray, gray matter light gray.

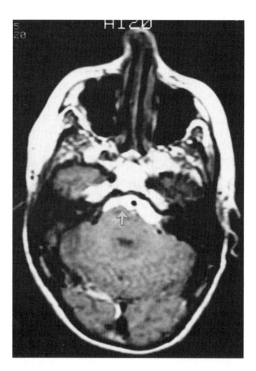

Figure 5.10   MRI, T₁ weighted image of a 25-year-old male with sudden onset headache. There is a white area anterior to the pons consistent with bleeding into the subarachnoid space. Notice no artifact from the petrous bones. (CT remains the modality of choice in patients with suspected intracranial blood.)

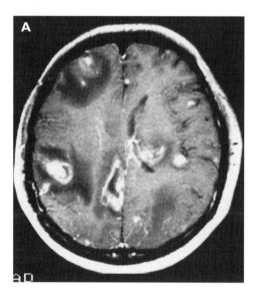

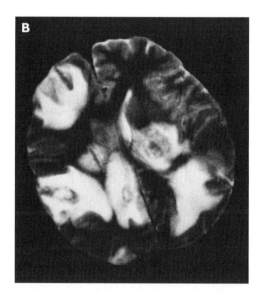

Figure 5.11   A 32-year-old male with AIDS presented with progressive headache and bilateral neurologic signs. A, MRI, T₁ weighted image reveals multifocal areas of decreased signal with mass effect on the ventricle. B, MRI, T₁ weighted following IV contrast. Small focal areas of enhancement with edema are consistent with toxoplasmosis.

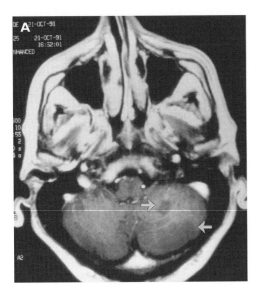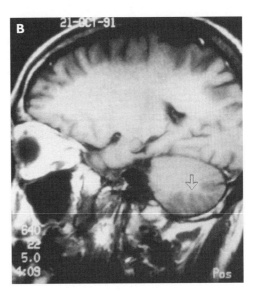

Figure 5.12   A 69-year-old male with sudden onset ataxia, a posterior headache, and negative CT scan. T₁ weighted axial MRI (*A*, horizontal; *B*, saggital) scans reveal multiple areas of infarction in the posterior fossa.

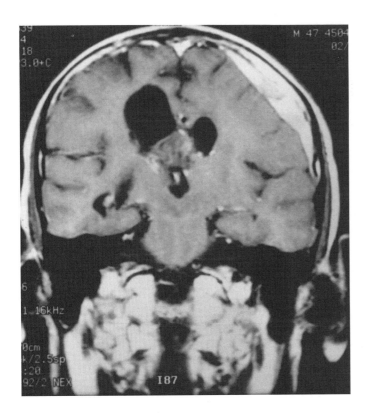

Figure 5.13   T₁ weighted MRI of a 52-year-old male with headache following a head injury. The patient also has a history of lung cancer. The scan reveals a white area on patient's left (right side of picture), consistent with a subdural hematoma. There is also a tumor in the midline which appears as a round lesion between the ventricles.

Various studies have suggested changes on MRI in migraine. Deep white matter foci have been reported in up to 40% of patients. In some cases these were identified independent of the type of migraine that occurred. There did not appear to be any correlation with age or sex of the patient, or duration or frequency of headache.

Two types of deep white matter foci were identified. These were seen either in periventricular white matter or deep within white matter. The etiology and significance of these changes are unknown and other studies have refuted these findings, suggesting that changes on MRI may not be as common as previously thought.

CEREBRAL ANGIOGRAPHY

Cerebral angiography remains the investigation of choice when vascular lesions such as arteriovenous malformation or aneurysms are suspected; however, its use is limited because of its invasiveness. MR angiography is a noninvasive tool and can often detect aneurysms and vascular abnormalities as small as 3 mm in diameter. If vascular abnormalities are suspected after a CT scan or MRI has been performed, cerebral angiography is often required.

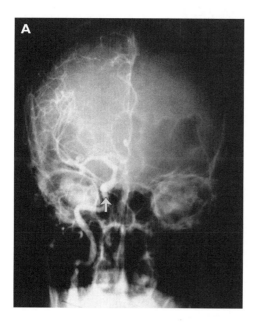 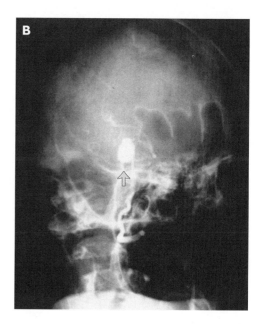

Figure 5.14 Cerebral angiograms of a 33-year-old female with headache of recent onset and a family history of intracranial aneurysm. A, A small cerebral aneurysm is visible in the right-middle cerebral artery (arrow). B, A larger basilar artery aneurysm (arrow) is also identified.

OTHER MODALITIES

In the clinical diagnosis of headache, the role of electroencephalography (EEG) is limited. Moreover, it is not recommended in the routine evaluation of migraine unless there is a suspicion of epilepsy or seizures.

Lumbar puncture should be used where the clinical symptoms suggest an infectious process (e.g., meningitis or encephalitis) or if subarachnoid hemorrhage is suspected and results of the CT scan are inconclusive. Lumbar puncture is also the investigation of choice to measure opening pressure if a pseudotumor is suspected.

In cases in which a mass lesion is suspected, the fundi cannot be clearly seen, or focal neurological deficits are present. CT scanning should be done initially to rule out mass effect prior to lumbar puncture to avoid brainstem herniation.

Bibliography

Alberico R, Patel M, Casey S, Jacobs B, Maguire W, Decker R. Evaluation of the circle of Willis with three dimensional CT angiography in patients with suspected intracranial aneurysms. Am J Neuroradiol 1995; 16:1571–1578.

De Benedittis G, Lorenzetti A, Sina C, Bernasconi V. Magnetic resonance imaging in migraine and tension-type headache. Headache 1995; 35:264–268.

duBoulay GH, Ruiz JS, Rose FC, Stevens JM, Zilkha KJ. CT changes associated with migraine. Am J Neuroradiol 1983; 4: 472–473.

Igarashi H, Sakai F, Kan S, Okada J, Tazaki Y. Magnetic resonance imaging of the brain in patients with migraine. Cephalalgia 1991; 11:69–74.

Osborn RE, Alder DC, Mitchell CS. MR imaging of the brain in patients with migraine headaches. Am J Neuroradiol 1991; 12:521–524.

Passier P, Vredeveld JW, de Krom M. Basilar migraine with severe EEG abnormalities. Headache 1994; 34:56–58.

Pavese N, Canapicchi R, Nuti A, Bibbiani F, Lucetti C, Collavoli P, Bonuccelli U. White matter MRI hyperintensities in a hundred and twenty-nine consecutive migraine patients. Cephalalgia 1994; 14:342–345.

Sand T. EEG in migraine: a review of the literature. Funct Neurol 1991; 6:7–22.

Supplementary Search Strategies

SuSS 1

Subject	explode Headache (index term)
Subject	explode Angiography (index term)
Limited to	Human
AND	1994 through 1997

SuSS 2

Subject	explode Headache (index term)
Subject	explode Magnetic Resonance Imaging (index term)
Limited to	Human
AND	1994 through 1997

Chapter 6

TENSION-TYPE HEADACHE

Nearly everyone, at some time or other, has had tension-type headaches. Though these headaches are very common, most people never seek medical care for them (in contrast to migraine), because they tend not to be very severe, they nearly always respond well to over-the-counter (OTC) analgesics, and their relationship to fatigue and emotional tension is usually evident. When someone with tension-type headaches consults a physician, it is often because the patient's insight into the connection between discontent and discomfort is lacking, because there is concern about underlying disease (such as a brain tumor or an aneurysm), or because the headaches are increasing in frequency or intensity and becoming resistant to OTC medication.

PATHOPHYSIOLOGY

The term "tension-type headache" reflects the longstanding belief of most physicians that the head pain is a somatic manifestation of psychological distress. A century ago, clinicians like Gowers and Romberg declared the basic problem with those suffering these headaches was "overintrospection" and "lack of diversion." Fifty years ago, Wolff's rather primitive electromyographic (EMG) studies suggested the head pain arose from psychologically determined involuntary spasm of scalp, neck, and shoulder muscles—so-called "muscle contraction headaches." While these theories probably apply to some people with tension-type headaches, there are many other patients with symptomatically identical headaches who appear to have no evident psychopathology and no EMG-demonstrable muscle spasm.

DIAGNOSIS

The International Headache Society (IHS), in its "Classification and Diagnostic Criteria," emphasize the recurrent and episodic nature of the headaches, their duration of several minutes to seven days, their usual mild to moderate (as opposed to severe) intensity, their bilaterality, their failure to be exacerbated by routine physical activities, and their lack of accompaniments such as nausea, vomiting, and phono- or photophobia. In many respects, these characteristics are the antitheses of migraine. Like migraine, though, there is the absolute requirement for the absence, on history and examination, of any evidence of a disease which might cause the headache.

The IHS classification attempts to distinguish between tension-type headaches associated with involuntary muscle contraction ("associated with disorder of pericranial muscles") and those which are not, on the basis of the presence or absence of increased tenderness and increased EMG activity in these muscles. It is not clear whether there is therapeutic utility in this distinction.

It also distinguishes between "episodic tension-type headaches" and "chronic tension-type headaches" on the basis of whether or not, in the preceding several months, the headache has persisted for at least 15 days out of each month. This does seem to be a useful prognostic distinction. People with "chronic tension-type headaches" are usually significantly encumbered with anxiety or depression, notoriously prone to excessive and ineffectual ingestion of medication, and definitely difficult to treat.

Those with chronic tension-type headaches are also liable to have occasional attacks of migraine, usually without aura. It is important, through good history, to dissect out the presence of these migrainous headaches, for the treatment of the two types is different. The statement that migraine without aura is indistinguishable from tension-type headache usually reflects inadequate effort expended in history-taking (see Chapter 8, *Migraine*). Many people with chronic tension-type headaches may also have medication-induced headaches, and these too should be identified by seeking in the history evidence of a clear temporal relationship between the ingestion of medication and the subsequent recurrence of headache, and by insistence upon having exact details of all medications taken by the patient (see Chapter 14, *Medication-Induced Headaches*).

In taking the history, look for a usual age of onset between the teens and the late thirties, and be suspicious of headaches beginning earlier or later, which (while they could be tension-type headaches) might represent disease. Ask about typical body postures at work and in the home, and when driving; in some cases postural muscle strain plays a role in causing headaches. Look for symptoms of depression (low mood, lack of enjoyment of life, sleep disturbance, impaired libido) and of anxiety (irritability, preoccupation, sleep disturbance, somatic symptoms such as palpitations and sweating, and "general angst") and seek out factors in the domestic, school, or occupational environment which might be contributing to these.

Sometimes, the question, "What do *you* think is causing your headaches?" elicits a revealing answer.

Examination may show some tautness and tenderness of the scalp, neck, and shoulder muscles, though the significance of these is often a matter of fine judgment. Similarly, the neck movements (active or passive) may be restricted by muscular stiffness and discomfort. There should be no other abnormal findings on examination; anything else is a "demand bid" for investigation to seek out disease as a cause of the headache.

In theory, imaging such as CT scan or MRI should not be necessary with a typical history of tension-type headaches and a normal physical examination. Some of these patients, however, are so anxious and so concerned about themselves that an imaging procedure may be necessary to settle their fears and to bring them to a point where they are psychologically ready to begin treatment.

TREATMENT

As always, explanation, education and reassurance form the mainstay of therapy. It is folly to simply write these people a prescription for a tranquilizer or an antidepressant; this gets the patient out of the office, but it does not get the headache out of the patient. The patient needs to know what the presumed mechanism of the headache is ("muscle strain caused by fatigue, worry, stress, poor posture, and lack of exercise" usually works better than "you are neurotic"), and needs to "buy into" a rational and coordinated plan to correct the problem. An empathetic family physician can use this opportunity to give some highly useful informal psychotherapy. Referral to a psychiatrist should seldom be necessary, and unless the patient is carefully prepared for this, the referral may be counterproductive.

Physical measures can be quite useful. At their simplest, they may involve paying attention to posture, correcting slouching and the "head forward while you work" position, and encouraging the patient to get up and stretch every half hour. Having the patient or someone else knead the scalp and neck muscles for 10 minutes two or three times per day, and standing under a hot shower with the water spraying on the head and neck for 10 minutes every night is a natural extension of this homemade physiotherapy. More intractable or more affluent patients can graduate to formal massage therapy, full-scale physiotherapy, or muscle-monitored biofeedback. It is unclear why these physical measures can be so effective, given the paucity of evidence that the muscles really are the cause of the headaches. Maybe the muscles *are* responsible. Or perhaps these are just various ways of inducing relaxation.

Critical Decisions

A Tension-type headache
- Recurrent and episodic, mild-to-moderate severity.
- Duration of several minutes to 7 days.
- Bilateral, frontal.
- No associated symptoms of nausea, vomiting, photophobia.

B Presence of concomitant symptoms
- History should include questions regarding body postures at work and when driving.
- Symptoms of depression (mood, energy, sleep disturbance, anorexia).
- Factors in the home, school, and work setting that may be a source of stress.

C Examination
- Examination may demonstrate taut, tender scalp and neck muscles
- Neck movement may be restricted
- Examination is otherwise normal

D Investigation
- Imaging with CT scan or MRI not necessary for tension-type with normal examination.
- When patients anxious about underlying disease, it may be necessary to settle their fears.

Differential Diagnosis of Chronic Tension-Type Headache

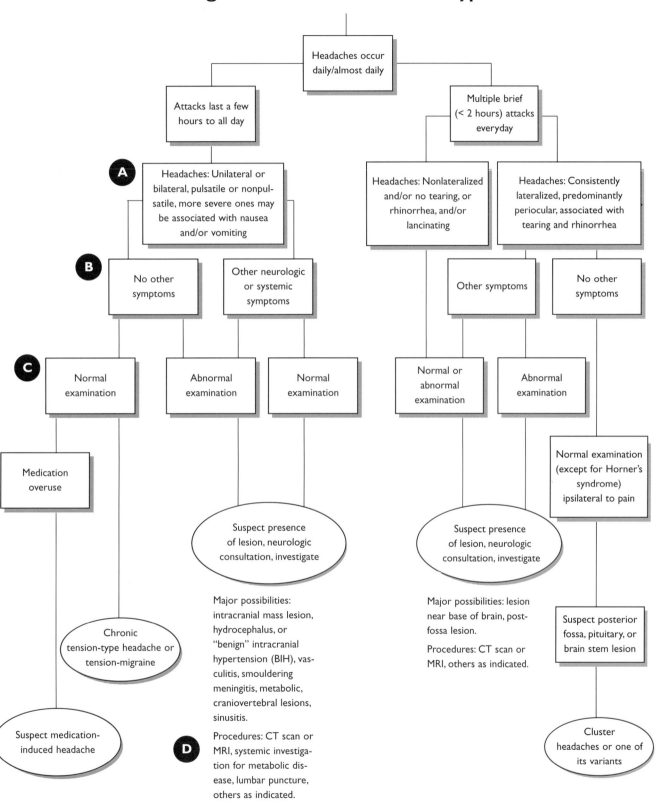

Ideally, medication should be minimized, for a number of reasons. First, though the fine strokes of the pathophysiology of tension-type headache are obscure, the broad outline of a lifestyle-related symptom seems clear. Therefore, it makes sense to try to alter the patient's somatic reaction to the emotional or physical environment; medication, which calls for no adjustment on the part of the patient, seems at best makeshift therapy. Second, people with chronic headaches are notoriously prone to develop problems with medications ranging from dependence to medication-induced headaches. Occasional use (no more often than 2 or 3 days in any week) of OTC analgesics for headaches which do not respond to physical measures is appropriate; recourse to stronger analgesics should be a rare and closely monitored event. Though combinations of analgesics with "muscle relaxants" are available, evidence of their efficacy in tension-type headaches is lacking, and their use is not recommended.

People with chronic tension-type headaches (occurring more often than 15 days per month) who show no response to physical measures may require prophylactic medication. If anxiety is prominent, a time-limited trial of low dose anxiolytic medication may be helpful; examples include diazepam 2.5 mg b.i.d. for 2 weeks, or lorazepam 0.5 mg b.i.d. for 2 weeks. If anxiety is not a feature, if depression is present, and/or if there is a sleep disturbance, a tricyclic antidepressant is worth trying. Amitriptyline is, in the view of many headache specialists, the "silver bullet" for chronic tension-type headaches. It should be started in a small dose (10 to 25 mg at bedtime) in order to avoid side effects which could lead the patient to stop the medication, and slowly increased, aiming at a maintenance dose of 50 to 100 mg every night. The key advice with all tricyclics is "start low and go slow." Other tricyclics found useful for headaches in controlled studies include nortriptyline 25 mg b.i.d. to q.i.d., doxepin 10 to 125 mg q.h.s., and desipramine 25 to 125 mg q.h.s. For reasons that are unclear, the selective serotonin reuptake inhibitors (SSRIs) are not nearly as effective as the tricyclics for headache therapy.

SUMMARY

Tension-type headaches can be trying to treat, partly because the "menu" of available therapies, as compared with that for migraine, is limited. The general principles are those for the treatment of any type of headache:

1. Through a detailed history and a careful examination, ensure the diagnosis is correct. If there is any doubt, in your mind or the patient's, consider imaging.

2. Through careful explanation, "sell" the diagnosis to the patient.
3. With equal care, detail the treatment plan to the patient, indicating the reasons for the various measures, their anticipated benefits, and any adverse effects.
4. Start treatment of tension-type headaches with physical measures.
5. Emphasize that OTC analgesic use must be limited.
6. If all the above give insufficient benefit, try an anxiolytic if anxiety is prominent; otherwise, use amitriptyline in a "start low and go slow" mode.

Bibliography

Diamond S, Dalessio DJ. The practicing physician's approach to headache (5th ed.) Baltimore: Williams & Wilkins, 1992:122–137.

Olesen J, Tfelt-Hanson P, Welch KMA. The headaches. New York: Raven Press, 1993:437–542.

Tollison CD, Kunkel RS. Headache Diagnosis and Treatment. Baltimore: Williams & Wilkins, 1993:123–180.

Supplementary Search Strategies

SuSS 1

Subject	Tension Headache (index term)
Subject	explode Diagnosis (subheading)
Subject	Sensitivity and Specificity (index term)
Limited to	Human
AND	1994 through 1997

SuSS 2

Subject	Tension Headache (index term)
Limited to	Human
AND	Meta-Analysis (publication type) or Clinical Trial (publication type)
AND	1994 through 1997

Chapter 7

POST-TRAUMATIC AND CERVICOGENIC HEADACHES

Chronic headaches may be post-traumatic or cervicogenic in origin. There is controversy about the frequency, pathophysiology, and even the legitimacy of post-traumatic and cervicogenic headaches. Psychological factors may, or may not, play a compelling role in the genesis of these headaches, and both may or may not produce significant disability.

POST-TRAUMATIC HEADACHES

There is no doubt that severe head injury with its consequent brain damage may produce many neurologic symptoms and signs. What is at issue is the extent to which *minor* head or neck trauma results in headaches, other complaints, and disability. Consider the following typical story:

A previously healthy young man was stopped at an intersection when his car was hit from the rear by another automobile. The impact dented the rear bumper and trunk lid, causing minor damage. He was thrown backwards and then forward but was restrained by his seatbelt. He was dazed, and can't remember whether or not his head struck anything; there may have been a few seconds when he was not fully aware of his environment. He got out of his car and exchanged insurance information with the other driver. As he drove home, he became aware of a tight discomfort in his neck and in the back of his head, which over the next few hours became frank pain, and spread to involve the entire head. He felt nauseated and vaguely "dizzy." He slept poorly that night (and every night thereafter), and his headache was worse the next morning. He went to his local Emergency Department, where the only abnormal physical finding was a little tenderness of his neck, and some limitation of its range of movement in all planes; the results of cervical spine radio-graphs were normal; he was given a prescription for "pain-killers" and a "muscle relaxant."

Now, a year later, he continues to have daily diffuse headaches, and takes analgesics everyday. His headaches and "dizziness," and other symptoms which subsequently developed (irritability, difficulty concen-trating, memory impairment, fatigue) have led to his being put on long-term disability by his employer. His relationship with his wife and chil-dren has deteriorated because of his preoccupation with his symptoms, and he now sits around the house most of the day. He has consulted a succession of neurologists and has had normal results from neurologic examinations, CT scans and MRI, and repeat cervical spine radiographs. He has had a neuropsychological test battery that has been interpreted as suggesting "frontotemporal dysfunction" and depression.

Though such stories are frequent in the "automobile era," one can find them in the medical literature of the 1800s. Many of these cases involved patients seeking compensation from injuries sustained during railroad travel. Osler (1892) com-mented that only rarely did such cases ever turn out to have organic disease. He emphasized that, "so long as litigation is pending and the patient is in the hands of lawyers the symptoms usually persist. Settlement is often the starting point of a speedy and perfect recovery." His equally eminent contemporary, Gowers (1888), asserted that, "it is rare for symptoms to be purely mental. It is often asserted by those employed by railway companies, that symptoms quickly subside when the sufferer's claims are settled, but in a good many individuals whom I have had an opportunity of observing long after they had received … (compensation) … this subsidence had not occurred … ."

The controversy continues.

At one pole are those who stress the following points:

- Animal experiments indicate that even minimal and indirect head trauma may produce microscopic lesions (axonal injuries) in the brain.
- Sometimes the more sensitive neuroimaging procedures, such as single photon emission computed tomography (SPECT) scanning and MRI, show areas of abnormality.
- Neuropsychological test batteries often are interpreted as showing changes consis-tent with organic cerebral dysfunction.

- Most studies show that settling of litigation does not have any effect on the symptoms or on the clinical outcome.

At the other pole are those who point out that:

- There are no data from eventual autopsy studies on "post-traumatic syndrome" sufferers that have identified lesions as being responsible for their headaches.
- Precisely because SPECT and MRI are so sensitive, they display areas of "abnormality" in people who are asymptomatic: a recent research study in which community-dwelling persons older than 64 years had MRIs, showed that 95.6% had "white matter abnormalities."
- Neuropsychological studies are subject to shortcomings, such as that patients can be taught to give certain responses, that performance can be affected by emotional state, and that interpretation is subjective enough that it is not uncommon for a psychologist on the defendant's side to give a report diametrically opposed to the report of the plaintiff's psychologist.
- Symptoms identical to those found in the "post-traumatic syndrome" are found in about 5% of the general population who have never been injured: the emotional stress of trauma and/or the expectations and behavior engendered by litigation may bring out these latent neurotic symptoms in people who have been involved in accidents.
- These symptoms are extremely rare in professional athletes such as football players and race drivers, who frequently sustain injury.
- Although it is true that termination of litigation does not terminate the symptoms, it is also true that the symptoms do not arise following trauma, or do so only very rarely, in societies where there is no litigation.

Where does the truth lie? We do not know, and it is likely that even among the authors, given the aforementioned data, different conclusions would be drawn. There are, however, a few considerations that may be helpful in managing these vexatious problems.

It is not at all unusual, following a direct or indirect ("whiplash") injury to the head, to have a headache for a few hours or days. The reason for this is obscure; maybe it is due to stretching of muscles and ligaments in the neck, with referral of pain to the head. When seen early following trauma, patients need to be reassured that this headache is to be expected, and will pass. They should also be reassured that a little dizziness and nausea, and sometimes even some vomiting, is par for the course. Analgesics should be prescribed in good doses, but not for a long time, and application of local heat to the neck and head (as in standing under a long, hot

Critical Decisions

A **Reassure, inform, and explain**
- Emphasize risks of chronic medication
- Discourage use of pills and encourage use of physical measures, relaxation, etc.
- Encourage return to normal activities.

B **Post-traumatic migraine**
- Response to treatment usually better than with nonmigrainous post-traumatic headaches.
- Use standard antimigraine therapy (see Chapter 8).

C **Medication-induced headaches**
- Some "chronic post-traumatic headaches" are actually medication-induced headaches and will respond to appropriate therapy (see Chapter 13).

D **The "post-traumatic syndrome"**
- Other symptoms accompany the headaches, such as memory disturbance, emotional lability, dizziness, etc.
- Poor prognosis.
- Often requires multispecialty approach.
- Refer early.

E **Physical therapy**
- Prescribe for a limited period; "forever physiotherapy" may engender chronic illness behavior.

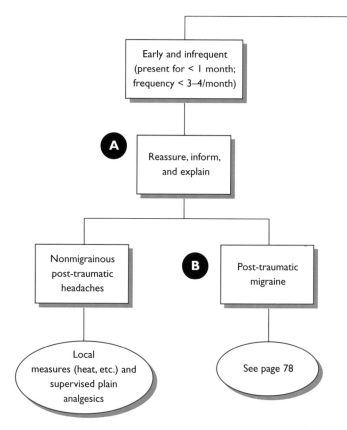

Post-Traumatic Headaches

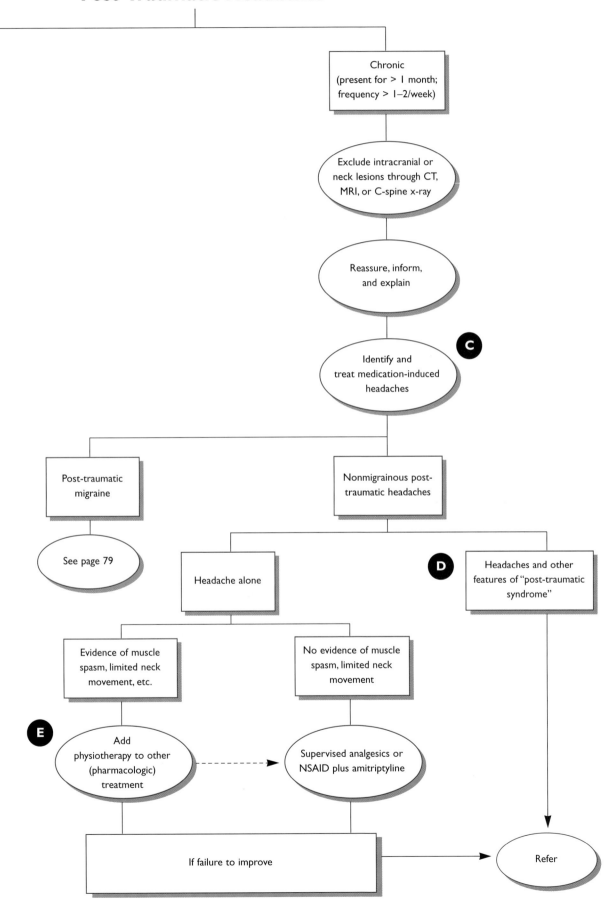

shower morning and night) can be recommended. Neck radiographs and other studies are rarely necessary; however, they should be gotten out of the way quickly, and the patient should be reassured that the findings are perfectly normal.

Sometimes, direct or indirect trauma appears to trigger headaches characteristic of migraine. This is more likely to occur in patients known to be migrainous, but "post-traumatic migraine" can be unveiled for the first time shortly after an accident. These headaches respond well to migraine treatment, so it is crucial to recognize them as migraine and initiate treatment quickly.

If post-traumatic headaches, especially the nonmigrainous ones, persist (or are allowed to persist) more than a couple of months, some adverse factors may enter the picture. Analgesic rebound headaches may contaminate the situation and, unrecognized, perpetuate the headaches. Frequent headaches may precipitate depression which, unrecognized and untreated, may declare itself as "more headaches." The use of amitriptyline or similar medication can be decisive at this point. Issues of justification and vindication may arise; an employer (or a physician) who overtly or otherwise conveys to the patient that his or her symptoms are "neurotic" or "imaginary" may evoke from the patient the exhibition of continuing and worsening symptoms as evidence that the disability is "real." The receiving of disability benefits or the commencement of litigation signals a poor outcome perhaps because only the most severe and "organic" of post-traumatic patients ever reach this point.

Assuming that migraine and depression have been identified and treated, and that the rare "lesional" causes of post-traumatic headaches such as hydrocephalus, chronic subdural hematoma, and low-pressure headaches from occult CSF leak have been ruled out through consultation and investigation, the following relationships exist between duration of post-traumatic headaches and prognosis:

- A majority of post-traumatic headaches clear within a few weeks, particularly if headache is the only symptom.
- Headaches that persist or recur for longer than two months are more likely to be associated with other symptoms, and to persist for at least some months more.
- At six months, it is more likely than not that the symptoms will not clear.
- At one year, it becomes extremely likely that the symptoms will never clear.
- At two to four years, depending on the series, the symptoms may be deemed permanent.

Are the headaches truly post-traumatic ? The answer lies not in the severity of the trauma—because symptoms may follow even the most trivial injury—nor in the characteristics of the headache—for post-traumatic headaches can take many forms. The keys are two: similar symptoms must not have existed prior to the trauma, and the new symptoms must follow the trauma by a credibly short interval. The International Headache Society's diagnostic criteria (1988) hold that symptoms must appear within two weeks of the trauma, though many experts would tighten this down to no more than a few days.

Are these post-traumatic headaches caused by a lesion such as subdural hematoma or hydrocephalus? Most will not be, but the rarity of the occurrence will be scant consolation for the patient, or the physician, if these dangerous and treatable lesions are missed. Features of the headache that suggest increased intracranial pressure, such as changing with posture, worsening with straining, or early morning exacerbation, are not typical of post-traumatic headaches, and suggest the need for referral and/or investigation. The presence of any abnormal neurologic sign is a "demand bid" for investigation.

Are these post-traumatic headaches migraine? The appearance de novo of migraine, or the reactivation of previously resolved migraine, following trauma are common occurrences. Post-traumatic migraine, unlike other types of post-traumatic headache, responds well to antimigraine therapy.

Is there analgesic abuse? Could some or all of these headaches now be medication-induced? Look for a history of regular intake of analgesics, with worsening of headaches correlating with times most removed from the last dose; consider a trial of withdrawal of analgesics.

Is the patient depressed? Look for a morose or flattened affect, and for symptoms such as sleep disturbance and fatigue that are consistent with depression. Consider a trial of antidepressant medication.

Should the patient be referred for management of post-traumatic headaches?

Once it has been established that these are post-traumatic headaches, that there is no lesion, and that fairly readily correctable factors such as migraine, depression, and medication-induced headaches are not in the picture, what should you do with the patient? These are complex management problems, and it may be that a specialist experienced with post-traumatic headache patients may be able to identify and head off complicating issues presented by these very difficult patients.

CERVICOGENIC HEADACHES

The issue of how important disease or dysfunction of the neck is as a cause of headache is complex and controversial. Certainly there are numerous pain-sensitive structures in the neck that can give rise to pain, including the eight pairs of cervical nerves and nerve roots, the synovial joints of the cervical spine, the annulus fibrosus of the intervertebral discs, the ligaments and muscles of the cervical spine, and the vertebral and carotid arteries which traverse the neck. Also, there are various pathways and mechanisms by which pain originating in at least the upper three or four cervical segments may be referred to the head, particularly (but not exclusively) the back of the head (see Chapter 3). Further, there are a few examples of unequivocal disease of the neck which present as headache. But, how often is headache a consequence of problems in the neck? How often do common neck conditions such as cervical disc disease cause headache? These are vexatious questions.

Some congenital bony anomalies of the craniovertebral junction, such as basilar invagination, atlanto-axial dislocation, and separate odontoid often produce headache, whether or not they are associated with soft tissue anomalies such as Arnold-Chiari malformation, Dandy-Walker syndrome, hydrocephalus, or syringomyelia. Typically, the headache is posterior, has a "bursting" quality, and is triggered by bending the neck or stooping forward, and relieved by lying down. It is believed to be due to stretching of the upper cervical nerve roots. Similar headaches have been reported in Arnold-Chiari malformation unassociated with bony craniovertebral anomalies; in this situation the headache may be due to hydrocephalus or to compression of the C-1 and C-2 nerve roots by the low-lying cerebellar tonsils.

Acquired craniovertebral junction lesions are also regularly associated with occipital pain. Tumors of the upper cervical region (e.g., meningiomas of the foramen magnum, ependymomas of the upper cervical cord) can stretch the upper cervical roots, as may the basilar invagination associated with Paget's disease of the skull. Rheumatoid arthritis and ankylosing spondylitis of the cervical spine, through fraying of ligaments, can produce atlanto-axial subluxation which results in headache and nastier complications such as impaling the upper cervical spine with the odontoid process on forward head movements. Paget's disease, metastatic tumor, or osteomyelitis of the skull or upper cervical spine may produce periosteal pain which can be translated into headache.

All of these are rare. Cervical disc disease (cervical spondylosis) is common, and is commonly blamed for causing headaches. But is this true? The problems with attributing headaches to cervical spondylosis include the following:

- Cervical spondylosis most often involves the lower cervical vertebrae, from which there are no apparent pathways for referral of pain to the head.
- Many people with extensive and severe degenerative cervical disc disease do not complain of headache.
- When headache disappears following medical treatment of cervical disc disease, this cannot be adduced as evidence of a causal relationship because many of the medications used to treat cervical disc disease (e.g., NSAIDs) are also efficacious for primary syndromes such as migraine and tension-type headaches.

A reasonable solution to this dilemma is to look for other causes for headache in a patient with cervical spondylosis unless there is clear evidence of involvement of the upper cervical vertebrae.

The issue of whether "whiplash" of the neck produces headache has been addressed in part in the first section of this chapter, but requires expansion here. Some authorities proclaim whiplash injury (forceful extension, then flexion of the neck, usually occasioned by a rear-end collision) to be one of the most frequent causes of chronic headaches. They invoke such difficult-to-prove mechanisms as traumatically produced compression or stretching of the upper cervical nerve roots, hypermobility (or sometimes hypomobility) of the cervical joints, micro-trauma to the brain stem and/or upper spinal cord, and the induction of fibrositis in the muscles of the scalp and neck. As evidence of the whiplash origin of the headaches, these authorities point to the occipital preponderance of many of these headaches, the worsening of the headache by neck movements, the abnormalities of movement of the neck (too little or too much) that may accompany such headaches, the finding of muscle spasm or nodules or "trigger points" in muscles which when pressed reproduce the headache, the (often transient) relief of such headaches by injection of nerves or muscles in the neck, and the occasional finding of radiologic features such as loss of the normal lordosis or osteophytes of the cervical spine.

Cases of chronic headache due to neck injury clearly exist; what is not clear is how common they are.

Cervicogenic headache, a new term introduced in the European literature, is interpretable in two ways. One is that headache may be caused by a number of diseases involving the neck: craniovertebral pathology, spondylosis, and some forms of trauma. Few would argue with this. The other, more controversial, sense is that cervicogenic headache is a specific disease entity, a "morbus sui generis," characterized by a symptom complex of episodic unilateral headache often associated with nausea and vomiting and regularly associated with signs of neck involvement, such as provocation by neck movements or association with neck and shoulder pain, all stemming from a dysfunction of the neck that might have its origin in recent or remote trauma. Many authorities question this concept, and some have suggested that at least some cases of cervicogenic headache, defined in this sense, are migraine.

The critical decision to be made is whether a given headache is caused by disease or dysfunction of the neck. The International Headache Society, in its Classification and Diagnostic Criteria (1988), proposes the following as indicating that a headache may originate in the neck:

- Pain originating in, or predominantly involving, the neck and occiput; it may radiate to other parts of the head.
- Pain precipitated or aggravated by specific neck movements or by sustained neck postures.
- On examination, at least one of the following : resistance to or limitation of passive neck movements; changes in contour, consistency or tone of neck muscle, or in its response to stretching or contraction; abnormal tenderness of neck muscles.
- On neck radiographs, at least one of the following: abnormalities of movement in flexion or extension; abnormal posture; evidence of distinct pathology, excluding common changes such as spondylosis.

These seem reasonable. Patients with these features should be referred to an appropriate specialist for treatment of primary pathology, accessing of further investigation, arrangement of physical therapy, and provision of specific medical treatment.

Supplementary Search Strategy

SuSS I	
Subject	explode Headache (index term)
Subject	explode Wounds and Injuries (index term) or post-traumatic (text word) or post-traumatic (text word)
Limited to	Human
AND	Meta-Analysis (publication type) or Clinical Trial (publication type)
AND	1994 through 1997

Bibliography

Alves WM, Colohan ART, O'Leary TJ, et al. Understanding posttraumatic symptoms after minor head injury. J Head Trauma Rehab 1986; 1:1–12.

Barnsley L, Lord S, Bogduk N. Whiplash injury. Pain 1994; 58:283–307.

Brenner C, Friedman AP, Merritt HH, Denny-Brown D. Posttraumatic headache. J Neurosurg 1944; 1:379–382.

Caveness WF. Posttraumatic headaches. In: Caveness WF, Walker AE, eds. Head injury conference proceedings. Philadelphia: JB Lippincott, 1966:208–219.

Dikman S, McLean A, Temkin N. Neuropsychological and psychosocial consequences of mild head injury. J Neurol Neurosurg Psychiatry 1986; 49:1227–1232.

Edmeads J. The cervical spine and headache. Neurology 1988; 38:1874–1878.

Fredriksen TA, Hovdal H, Sjaastad O. Cervicogenic headache: clinical manifestations. Cephalalgia 1987; 7:147–160.

Gennarelli TA, Thibault LE, Adams JH, et al. Diffuse axonal injury and traumatic coma in the primate. Ann Neurol 1982; 12:564–574.

Gowers WR. Diseases of the nervous system. Philadelphia: P Blakiston, Son & Co., 1888:439–440.

Headache Classification Committee of the International Headache Society. Classification and diagnostic criteria for headache disorders, cranial neuralgias and facial pain. Cephalalgia 1988; 8(suppl 7):1-97.

Jacobson SA. Mechanism of the sequelae of minor craniocervical trauma. In: Walker AE, Caveness WF, et al., eds. Late effects of head injury. Springfield, IL: Thomas, 1969:501–526.

Kelly RE. Post-traumatic headache. In: Vinken PJ, Bruyn GW, eds. Handbook of clinical neurology. 48 (Headache). Amsterdam: Elsevier Science Publishers, 1988:383–390.

Maimaris C, Barnes MR, Allen MJ. Whiplash injuries of the neck: a retrospective study. Injury 1988; 6:393–396.

McRae DL. Bony abnormalities at the craniospinal junction. Clin Neurosurg 1969; 16:356–375.

Osler W. The principles and practice of medicine. New York: D. Appleton and Company, 1892:981.

Packard RC. Posttraumatic headache: permanency and relationship to legal settlement. Headache 1992; 32:496–500.

Packard RC, Ham LP. Posttraumatic headache: determining chronicity. Headache 1993; 33:133–134.

Pfaffenrath V, Dandekar R, Pollmann W. Cervicogenic headache—the clinical picture, radiologic findings and hypotheses on its pathophysiology. Headache 1987; 27:495–499.

Povlishock JT, Becker DP, Cheng CLY, et al. Axonal change in minor head injury. J Neuropath Exp Neurol 1983; 42:225–242.

Schrader H. Natural evolution of late whiplash syndrome outside the medicolegal context. Lancet 1996; 347:1207–1211.

Warner JS, Fenichel GM. Chronic post-traumatic headache often a myth? Neurology 1996; 46:915–916.

Weiss HD, Stern BJ, Goldberg J. Post-traumatic migraine: chronic migraine precipitated by minor head or neck trauma. Headache 1991; 31:451–456.

Chapter 8

MIGRAINE

CLINICAL PRESENTATION

Migraine is a syndrome of episodic headache, often unilateral, which is associated with nausea, vomiting, photo- or phonophobia. There may or may not be an aura.

Migraine occurs more commonly in women than in men by a ratio of 2 or 3 to 1. A family history of migraine is present in more than 60% of cases. Attacks commonly begin to occur between adolescence and the early twenties. Although the onset of migraine may be after age 40, this is unusual and may warrant investigations beyond the history and physical examination.

Prodrome

There may be a prodrome to the attack. Prodromal symptoms can include depression or elation, polydipsia and polyuria or fluid retention, diarrhea or constipation, chills, fatigue, and/or pallor. Many patients experience food cravings prior to the attack; if they indulge these, when the attack follows, the food may be mistakenly implicated as a "migraine trigger."

Aura

About 15% of migraineurs experience an aura. In these patients, the aura may occur with only a few attacks, most attacks, or all attacks. Typically, the aura precedes the headache, lasts 20 to 60 minutes, and then clears before the headache begins. However, the aura may trespass into the first several minutes of the headache. Most auras are visual and take a variety of forms including scintillating saw-toothed crescents of light that drift across the visual fields, glistening points of light (photopsias) or shimmering heat-wave-like obscurations (Figure 8.1). Some auras are sensory, consisting of tingling and numbness, typically originating in the

Figure 8.1   Variations of visual aura, including lace patterns and heat wave-like obscurations

mouth and in the hand, and sometimes spreading through one half of the body. Rarely, monoparesis, hemiparesis, dysphasia, or other cognitive changes may comprise the aura; when aura symptoms are this atypical, it is prudent to be on guard against migraine mimics such as transient ischemic attacks or seizures.

Nature of Pain

Although migraine headaches typically are unilateral and anterior, they may be bilateral or posterior and may in some patients or in some attacks involve the jaw or cheek. The duration of headache varies, often depending on the rapidity with which treatment is given, and its efficacy. Typically, a headache lasts from 4 to 72 hours. It is a throbbing, pulsatile pain that often is severe, though moderate or even mild attacks of migraine headache are not uncommon even in the same patient; failure to recognize this variability may result in milder attacks of migraine being misdiagnosed. The headache is worsened by (or in some cases triggered by) exertion, and is eased by resting quietly with the head slightly elevated.

Concomitant Symptoms

Migraine headaches are accompanied by other features which may include anorexia, nausea, vomiting, diarrhea, aversion to light (photophobia), aversion to noise (phonophobia), aversion to smells (osmophobia), chilliness, goose bumps, quivering, and profound malaise. Complete absence of accompaniments in a migraine attack is rare. Failure to elicit their presence should prompt consideration of another diagnosis.

Neurologic Examination

The neurologic examination during and between attacks is normal; if it is not, the diagnosis of migraine is likely wrong. During an attack there may be general physical abnormalities including tachycardia, increased blood pressure, pallor, and sweating, representing autonomic responses to pain. Also, as local accompaniments of the migraine attack there may be tenderness of the scalp and neck muscles, and soreness and distention of the blood vessels of the scalp. Compression of these vessels by finger pressure may temporarily relieve or shift the pain of the headache.

Following an attack there is often a "postdrome" consisting of great fatigue, general "fragility," and desire to sleep. This sleep may be quite restorative, so that on awakening the patient may rebound into his or her previous energetic self.

Migraine Triggers

Attacks of migraine may occur "out of the blue," but may also be triggered by a variety of psychological, hormonal, dietary, and environmental factors. Curiously, it is not so much stress, as release from stress, that seems to precipitate many migraine attacks; this may be why weekends are a favorite time for migraine to occur. Both oversleeping and sleep deprivation have been repaid with migraine, suggesting that disruption of normal patterns is responsible. In children, even happy excitement, like attending one's birthday party, may result in a migraine, and many a migrainous bride has had a headache on her wedding day.

Migraine occurring regularly as a prelude or accompaniment to menstruation (and sometimes ovulation) is well known, as is the cessation of migraine in many of these same women during pregnancy. Oral contraceptive medication may worsen migraine, but almost as often it either has no effect or even improves it.

Various foods have been implicated, with varying validity, as migraine triggers. There is little doubt that alcohol, especially red wine and colored liquors, may either trigger migraine or worsen an attack in progress. Chemical additives, such as monosodium glutamate, aspartame, and nitrites (added to some smoked meats to preserve color) can precipitate migraine in some patients. Chocolate, aged cheeses,

nuts, citrus fruit, and dairy products have all been implicated by some as factors precipitating their attacks. Caffeine, or more particularly the missing of a regular dose of caffeine by "coffee hounds" or "cola freaks," often may precipitate a migraine attack.

Environmental influences which may be important in triggering migraine include strong odors such as perfume, aftershave lotion, cigarette smoke, and cooking odors. Changes in barometric pressure, heralding a change for the worse in the weather, may unleash migraine attacks in many people.

A "full house" migraine attack, therefore, consists of a triggering influence, a prodrome, an aura, a headache with its accompaniments, and a postdrome, all occurring in an individual with a normal neurologic examination. Such an attack is instantly recognizable as migraine. A full house, however, is as rare in migraine as it is in poker. Usually, the patient presents just with a headache and one or two other features. By obtaining detailed descriptions of many attacks and by conducting a careful neurologic examination, the physician can still make a confident diagnosis of migraine, and on this foundation build successful therapy.

Identification and Elimination of Migraine Triggers

While medications can be quite effective in treating acute attacks of migraine (episodic treatment), or in preventing them (prophylactic treatment), they all can cause side effects. Before starting these, therefore, the physician should inquire into what factors seem to trigger the patient's migraine attacks (see page 75), in hopes that eliminating these triggers may reduce both the frequency of headaches and the need for medication.

TREATMENT OF MIGRAINE

Headache Diary

A useful prelude to treatment with medication is to have the patient keep a "headache diary." This need not be elaborate; notations on the kitchen calendar will do, as long as they are accurate and complete. The doctor needs to know: (a) how many headaches occurred in that month; (b) how long each lasted; (c) how severe each one was (instruct the patient in a simple grading system); (d) what factors (such as menstruation, food, etc.) seemed implicated; (e) what medication was taken (identity and amount of medication); and (f) with what effects (both beneficial and adverse). This information provides a baseline against which to measure improvement. It may reveal patterns of which the patient was unaware, and it may give early warning of medication overuse.

Episodic Treatment

A. Physical and behavioral aspects

Most headache sufferers automatically do (or refrain from doing) certain things when they have an attack, but few know all these nonspecific "tricks" to ease headache pain, so it is worthwhile for the doctor to review them.

Migraine pain is worsened by movement, light, and noise; resting in a quiet, darkened room can lessen the pain. Keeping the head elevated at about 30 degrees may be more comfortable than lying perfectly flat. Cold applied to the head by an ice-pack, a cold wet towel, or a refrigerated gel pack can constrict the painfully dilated superficial scalp vessels and increase the pain threshold; paradoxically, a few migraineurs get more relief from heat. Pressure applied to the head by a towel or other cloth band tightly encircling it, may ease pain by collapsing distended vessels and by "counterirritation."

Various behavioral techniques for coping with pain may be useful in migraine. Whether they work by "taking the patient's mind off the pain" or by "recruiting cortically-originating descending antinociceptive pathways" is unclear. They include relaxation, biofeedback, meditation, imagery, and self-hypnosis. Most people can learn them, but few can use them successfully during an acute attack.

Acupuncture can sometimes relieve acute pain, including that of migraine; it is not often possible, however, to obtain acupuncture either on an urgent basis or for every headache. Injection of the nerves of the scalp, notably the occipital nerves, may sometimes relieve headache. Again, this procedure may not be available when needed. Moreover, if done too often (especially when corticosteroids are being injected along with the local anesthetic), there may be adverse effects.

In summary, things one can do for oneself may be of some use in mitigating the pain of migraine. For greater relief, most people rely on medications.

B. Analgesics

Over 90% of migraine sufferers take over-the-counter (OTC) analgesics such as acetylsalicylic acid (aspirin) or acetaminophen (Tylenol®). Some brands of these "simple analgesics" are compounded with caffeine. This may not be known to some who take them, and it may be important for those subject to developing headaches when withdrawing from caffeine (see Chapter 14, *Medication-Induced Headaches*). In Canada, these analgesics compounded with 8 mg of codeine (Tylenol with Codeine #1 ®, 222s®) are available OTC without prescription. OTC analgesics are adequate treatment for many people's migraine, especially when the attacks are mild to moderate. They are not very effective for severe attacks, and their overuse in vain attempts to quell severe migraine often leads to the development of medication-induced headaches (MIH). MIH is more likely to occur when the analgesics overused are taken in combination with caffeine and/or codeine. Those taking OTC analgesics should be made aware that: (a) overuse may produce chronic daily headaches; and (b) while OTC analgesics should not be consumed more frequently than 2 or 3 days in any one week, when they are taken, the dose should be adequate, that is, 1000 mg of either acetylsalicylic acid or acetaminophen. There is evidence that soluble or effervescent acetylsalicylic acid is considerably better absorbed than the traditional solid tablet, particularly if taken with a 10 mg tablet of metoclopramide; this combination may be useful even for more severe migraine headaches.

Acetaminophen, alone or with caffeine, and the NSAIDs have not been demonstrated to pose a risk to the fetus when used in pregnancy. Fetal risk from acetylsalicylic acid has not been excluded.

When migraine sufferers consult a doctor and receive a prescription, in 65% of cases that prescription is for an analgesic. Most frequently prescribed are acetaminophen with varying amounts (15, 30, and 60 mg) of codeine (Tylenol® with Codeine # 2, 3, and 4); acetylsalicylic acid or acetaminophen with caffeine, a barbiturate, and sometimes codeine (Fiorinal®, Fioricet®); and acetaminophen with a vasoconstrictor and a relaxant (Midrin®). All are effective, particularly for mild to moderate attacks. While they may be helpful for severe attacks of migraine, in the experience of many physicians the specific antimigraine drugs are more effective for more intense headaches. Midrin® is not very likely to produce MIH, but the other prescription analgesics have been implicated.

Butorphanol, available as a nasal spray, is a mixed agonist-antagonist of opioid receptors. It is an opiate, and though not a common occurrence, it can cause dependence and therefore must be prescribed and used with circumspection. Drowsiness and dysphoria are sometimes troublesome side effects. Taken sparingly, it can be useful in relieving acute attacks of migraine. For mild to moderate attacks, other medications are appropriate.

Fetal risk from codeine cannot be ruled out; no fetal risk has been demonstrated from meperidine, morphine, or butorphanol.

C. Specific antimigraine drugs

Ergotamine is a potent agent that arrests or reverses the painful dilatation and inflammation of cranial blood vessels that is responsible for the pain of migraine (see Chapter 3, *Practical Pathophysiology of Headache*). It is not an innocuous medication, and so its use is best reserved for moderate to severe attacks. This restriction may be difficult because ergotamine is most likely to be effective when taken early in an attack, before some sufferers have formed their assessment of whether this attack is going to stay mild or become nasty. Because of its powerful vasoconstrictive property, ergotamine should not be used in patients who have conditions in which vascular insufficiency is believed to play a role, such as ischemic heart disease, hypertension, peripheral vascular disease, and Raynaud's phenomenon. The vasoconstriction produced by ergotamine may be heightened in the presence of infection, which is thus another contraindication to its use. Since ergotamine is degraded in the liver and excreted by the kidney, it is contraindicated in people with hepatic or renal dysfunction. Like most antimigraine drugs, it is contraindicated in pregnancy. Ergotamine is a very large molecule, and one of its side chains may combine with dopamine receptors to produce nausea and vomiting, which is a major consideration in a condition like migraine, where nausea and vomiting are either present, or in the wings, waiting to enter.

Despite all the contraindications and possible side effects noted above, and despite the fact that there are really no well-designed studies in the literature strongly attesting to its efficacy, ergotamine is a very useful drug, particularly in the hands of a physician who knows how to prescribe it and a patient who knows how to take it. When nausea and vomiting are problems, ergotamine can be given compounded with an antinauseant (e.g., Cafergot-PB®, Gravergol®), and just as important, in a reduced dose. When absorption by mouth is a problem (i.e., inefficacy by that route), ergotamine can be given as a rectal suppository, as a sublingual tablet, or as an orally inhaled spray (though this last formulation is difficult to find).

Dihydroergotamine (DHE) is a little different than ergotamine in that it is not as powerful an arterial constrictor, though it is just as likely to cause nausea or vomiting. Its usefulness lies in its availability as a subcutaneous or intramuscular injection (which a patient can be trained to self-administer, or which can be given in a doctor's office), and as an intravenous injection (best reserved for use in the Emergency Department—see Chapter 15, *Emergency Management of Acute Headaches*). DHE in a nasal spray formulation has been released in Canada, and its approval for use in the United States is said to be imminent. When injecting DHE, especially intravenously, it is prudent to precede it with an antinauseant, but this is unnecessary with the nasal spray. There are several studies in the literature which attest to the efficacy of DHE in its various formulations, for treating moderate to severe attacks of migraine. The side effect profile and the contraindications are similar to those for ergotamine.

Dosages for the various forms of ergotamine and DHE are shown in Table 8.1.

Sumatriptan is a newer medication which, like ergotamine and DHE, stimulates the serotonin 5-HT$_{1D}$ receptors to produce cranial vasoconstriction and reduce vascular inflammation, but unlike ergotamine and DHE it has no affinity for dopaminergic and adrenergic receptors and thus does not cause nausea, vomiting, or systemic vasoconstriction. It has proven to be quite efficacious in relieving attacks of migraine headache. Its shortcomings are few: its half-life is short and thus repeat dosing may be necessary in about 25% of attacks; in a small percentage of cases it has caused chest pain which, while not proven to come from the heart, has raised concerns; and it is expensive. It has the same contraindications as ergotamine and DHE, and because they stimulate the same serotonin receptor, the use of these different agents in close succession has been deemed inadvisable. Most neurologists reserve sumatriptan for use in moderate to severe migraine attacks.

Sumatriptan (Imitrex® in North America, Imigran® in Europe) is available in 25, 50, and 100 mg oral formats, depending on which country it is marketed in, and in 6 mg vials for self-administered subcutaneous injection. The injection is preferred for attacks that are accompanied by severe nausea or by vomiting. A nasal format of sumatriptan has recently been released in Canada (5 or 20 mg dose per squirt). Recommended dosage schedules for sumatriptan are shown in Table 8.1.

Table 8.1   Pharmacologic Treatment of Acute Attack of Migraine with Specific Antimigraine Agents

Medication	Strength & Route	Dosage	Side Effects
Ergotamine	1 mg oral tabs	2 at onset; then 1 q1/2h prn; max 6 tablets	Nausea Vomiting Cramping Ischemia
Ergotamine	2 mg sublingual	1 at onset; then 1 q1/2h prn; max 3 tablets	"
Ergotamine	2 mg suppository	1/2–1 at onset; then 1 in 1 hr prn	"
DHE DHE	1 mg/ml; SQ, IM, IV 0.5 mg/spray (nasal)	0.5–1.0 mg; rep in 1 hr prn 1 spray in each nostril; rep in 15 minutes (total dose=2 mg/attack)	As with ergotamine Flushing Giddiness
Sumatriptan	25, 50, & 100 mg oral	1 tablet (usually 50 mg); rep in 1 hr if relief fades (max. 300 mg/24hr)	Flushing
Sumatriptan Sumatriptan	6 mg/ml SQ injection 20 mg/spray (nasal)	1 ml SQ; rep in 1 hr if relief fades 1 spray; rep in 1 hr if relief fades	Tingling Chest discomfort

Treatment of ultrasevere migraine attacks

Using the paradigm of OTC analgesics, Midrin® or NSAIDs for mild attacks, combination analgesics or Midrin® or specific antimigraine drugs (sumatriptan, ergotamine, or DHE) for moderate attacks, and specific antimigraine drugs or butorphanol nasal spray for severe attacks, the great majority of migraine headaches can be handled. Occasionally, a patient will have an ultrasevere attack that fails to respond to these medications, and one must resort to extraordinary treatments such as intravenous DHE, intravenous narcotics, and/or intravenous neuroleptics. (See Chapter 15, *Emergency Management of Acute Headaches* for details.)

Critical Decisions

(A) Metoclopramide
- 10 mg given by direct IV injection over 2–3 min.
- May be given in 50 mL of normal saline and infused over 15 min. prior to DHE injection.
- Each metoclopramide dose should be administered 15 min. prior to DHE injection.
- Acute extrapyramidal side effects may occur, such as dystonia or akathisia.
- Oculogyric crisis may occur; benztropine mesylate (Cogentin) 1 mg IM/IV injection is effective in terminating this unusual adverse event.

(B) Dihydroergotamine
- 0.5 mg direct IV push slowly over 2–3 min., or may be diluted in 50 mL normal saline and given as an infusion over 20–30 min.
- May be repeated in an outpatient setting every hour until headache relieved, or to a maximum of 3 mg/24h.

- **Do not** use DHE in patients with ischemic heart disease, peripheral vascular disease, within 24 hours of sumatriptan, or if hypertension or chest pain occurs after the 0.5 mg test dose.

(C) Persistent migraine
- DHE can be repeatedly administered on an inpatient basis to patients who:
  - fail to respond to therapy,
  - present with status migrainosus (intractable migraine > 72 hours)
  - migraine superimposed upon chronic daily headache with or without analgesic, or
  - ergotamine rebound.

(D) Persistent migraine with nausea
- DHE can be administered every 8 hours for 2 days.
- A 3–5 day course may be beneficial for patients whose response is less than complete after the initial two-day trial.

Frequent Migraines

D. Prophylactic treatment

These medications are taken each day, whether or not the patient has an attack that day, in hopes of reducing the frequency of headaches. Migraine attacks unresponsive to attempts to identify and remove triggers, and to reasonable doses of episodic medication, should be occurring at least three times per month to justify the cost and possible side effects of prophylactic medication. If there are only one or two migraine attacks per month but they are devastating in severity or duration, prophylaxis may be warranted.

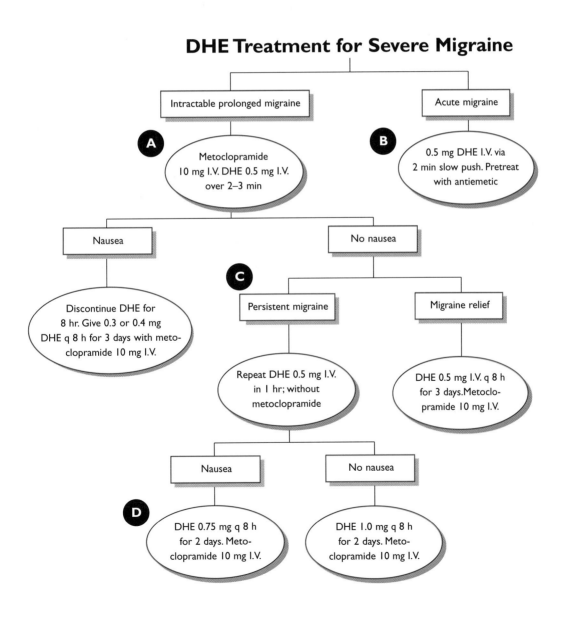

Most of these drugs useful in migraine prophylaxis were found serendipitous-ly; though proven efficacious in double-blind placebo-controlled studies, we still have no clear idea of why they work.

The medication most appropriately employed first as a migraine prophylactic should be either a beta-blocker, a calcium channel blocker (calcium antagonist), or a tricyclic (see algorithm). An exception to this rule is for the patient whose migraine occurs predominantly with menstruation and/or ovulation. In such cases, when removal of triggers (including consideration of discontinuing oral contraceptives) and employment of appropriate "episodic treatment" have failed to bring adequate relief, a trial of NSAIDs taken in a prophylactic mode could be essayed. For example, naproxen 250 mg b.i.d. or piroxicam 10 mg daily could be given either every day month round, or for 7 days before each period and during the period. If after two or three cycles the prophylactic NSAID is clearly not working, then the menstrual migraine should be treated with "regular" migraine prophylactic medication (see algorithm).

E. Beta-blockers

Some (but not all) beta-blockers are effective migraine prophylactic drugs; those that are useful include propranolol, nadolol, metoprolol, atenolol and timolol. Propranolol was the first of these to be used, but nadolol is becoming more popular because, being less lipid-soluble and therefore less able to penetrate the central nervous system, it is less likely to produce drowsiness, depression, and other CNS side effects. These drugs need not be used in doses sufficient to cause beta-blockade in order to decrease the frequency of migraine attacks. They should be started in a low dose (e.g., nadolol 20 mg daily) and gradually increased to a medium dose (e.g., nadolol 40–80 mg b.i.d.). Eight to 12 weeks of treatment may be necessary before maximum benefit becomes apparent. Sometimes, higher doses (e.g., nadolol 120–160 mg b.i.d.) are necessary, and are attainable without side effects if approached gradually. The principle in using beta-blockers is the same for most migraine prophylactic agents: start low and go slow. Sometimes, the potential "side effects" of the beta-blockers may be used to advantage. For example, a hypertensive patient with migraine may benefit doubly from a beta-blocker, as may an anxious and tremulous migraineur. Other potential side effects pose contraindications. For example, asthmatics, insulin-dependent diabetics, and exercise addicts, all of whom depend for their well-being on their intrinsic sympathetic responses, should not be given beta-blockers.

F. Calcium channel blockers

Some (but not all) calcium channel blockers are useful in migraine prophylaxis, again for unclear reasons. In many cases, a worthwhile reduction in migraine frequency results from doses insufficient to cause clinically discernible cardiovascular effects. Verapamil and flunarizine have perhaps the best established efficacy, though nifedipine and diltiazem are also believed useful. Flunarizine (Sibelium®) is available in Canada but not in the United States. Flunarizine may be started, without need for a gradual increase, in the full dose of two 5 mg capsules every night; it may take 9 weeks or more to exert its full therapeutic effects. It is contraindicated in those with a personal or family history of depression, for it can produce severe depression. It may also cause weight gain, drowsiness, Parkinsonism, and (especially in the elderly) involuntary movements. The side effects of verapamil are less intense, comprising most often constipation. It can be started in a modest dose (e.g., 80 mg b.i.d.) and gradually raised to 80 mg t.i.d. Sometimes, after initial benefit in this dose range, ground is lost; it can be regained by increasing the dose to 120 mg t.i.d. A once-daily dose of a sustained-release preparation may be used, particularily if compliance is a problem. Calcium channel blockers are contraindicated in people with low blood pressure, heart failure, or arrhythmias; there is no proof of safety for their use in pregnancy.

G. Tricyclic antidepressants

Some (but not all) of the tricyclic antidepressants are effective migraine prophylactic agents, but their efficacy for migraine is not related to the affective state of the patient; euthymic patients get just as much benefit as depressed ones. Those found in controlled studies to be useful are amitriptyline and doxepin, but most neurologists find that nortriptyline is also valuable, and some use others such as desipramine and imipramine. The role of the SSRIs (selective serotonin reuptake inhibitors) such as fluoxetine (Prozac®) in migraine prophylaxis has not yet been clearly established. When using the tricyclics in migraine prophylaxis, the rule again is to start low and go slow. Another rule is to try to use the possible side effects to the patient's advantage; for example, the migraine patient who can't get to sleep or stay asleep at night could use the sedative side effect of a bedtime dose of amitriptyline, and the slow and depressed patient can use the "lift" of b.i.d. doses of nortriptyline. Usual useful doses of the tricyclics are amitriptyline 50–75 mg q.h.s., or nortriptyline 25 mg b.i.d. or t.i.d. It may take some weeks for these to attain their maximum antimigraine efficacy. The anticholinergic side effects of the tricyclics can limit their employment; these side effects are not as pronounced with nortriptyline as with some of the others. There is evidence of risk to the fetus when amitriptyline and nortriptyline are used in pregnancy; there is no evidence that doxepin is safe for use in pregnancy.

H. Combination therapy

Combinations of these drugs may be useful when, alone, the medications have been suboptimally effective (see algorithm). A tricyclic and a beta-blocker, or a calcium channel blocker and a tricyclic, frequently work. Combinations of calcium channel blockers and beta-blockers are, of course, contraindicated.

When the above drugs, alone or in combination, are not efficacious, they should be discontinued and other agents, such as pizotifen or valproate may be brought into play (see algorithm).

I. Other medications

Pizotifen (available in Canada and Europe as Sandomigran®) is believed to prevent migraine by blocking 5-HT$_2$ receptors. It is best prescribed in the Sandomigran DS® (double strength, or 1 mg) form, starting right away in a dose of 2 mg q.h.s., and increasing over a couple of weeks, as needed, to 3–5 mg q.h.s. The q.h.s. dosing is used to put the side effect of drowsiness to the patient's benefit in getting him or her off to sleep at night. Also, the h.s. timing may allow the patient to sleep through the postdose appetite surge that might otherwise lead to increased eating and weight gain. Sandomigran® has not been proven safe for use in pregnancy.

Recently, good studies have demonstrated that the anticonvulsant valproate (Depakene, Depakote®) can be an efficacious migraine prophylactic in doses of 500–2000 mg per day, again reached via the "start low and go slow" route. It may take many weeks for valproate to attain its full efficacy. Its side effect profile is low, and includes nausea, drowsiness, vague dizziness, and occasionally mild transient hair loss. It should not be used as a prophylactic in pregnancy.

When adequate trials (taken faithfully in the recommended doses for at least 10 weeks) of the above medications have failed to decrease the frequency of migraine attacks to an acceptable level, consideration should be given to using either methysergide or a monoamine oxidase inhibitor (see algorithm, stage 4).

Methysergide (Sansert®) is an extremely powerful migraine prophylactic, with efficacy that becomes established in days rather than weeks. It is seldom employed because of concern about side effects, notably vasoconstriction in the acute use, and the development of fibrotic syndromes (retroperitoneal fibrosis, pleuro-pulmonary fibrosis) in long-term use. Nevertheless, the acute side effects are rare, and the long-term ones are said to be preventable by never using the drug for more than 5 or 6 months at a time without coming off it between courses for a "rest period" of at least 30 days. For many headache specialists, methysergide is their secret weapon. It can be started in a dose of one tablet (2 mg) b.i.d., and quickly worked up to three or four tablets per day, usually taken with food to prevent GI irritation.

Another "secret weapon," but one best left for those highly experienced in its use, is the monoamine oxidase (MAO) inhibitor phenelzine (Nardil®). Why it works is unclear, but many headache specialists use it as their last resort. The side effects of MAO inhibitors are well known, and include vague dizziness, orthostatic hypotension, weakness, fatigue, dry mouth, blurred vision, urinary hesitancy, and constipation. Dangerous hypertensive crises may arise as a result of interactions with other drugs or with the tyramine present in certain foodstuffs. Generally speaking, patients should be referred to a headache specialist if use of either methysergide or phenelzine is contemplated.

Most other drugs used for migraine prophylaxis are worthless, but a clear exception to this is that some NSAIDs, notably naproxen and piroxicam, which may be useful in some women with menstrual and/or ovulatory headaches when given throughout the month in fairly low doses. In some cases, giving these drugs just for the week before and during menstruation suffices. For resistant menstrual migraine, various hormonal therapies may be tried—preferably by or in collaboration with a gynecologist or endocrinologist. These hormonal therapies range from a trial of discontinuing oral contraceptive medications to the prescribing of estrogen via various routes (oral, percutaneous), with or without progestogens.

Whatever drug is used, remember that migraine prophylaxis should not be a life sentence. Use the drug until the migraine has been under tight control for 3 or 4 months, and then gradually sneak the medication out from under the patient, slowly weaning him or her off. (An obvious exception is methysergide, which must be stopped at 5 or 6 months.) Often, the patient can *coast*, free of the prophylactic medication and relatively free of migraine, for months.

Worst-Ever Headache

"The worst headache ever" occasionally is brought to the doctor's office by a known migraine sufferer. Almost always, this headache too is a migraine attack. Every once in a long while, though, it turns out to be a leaking aneurysm, a tumor, or some other nasty lesion (Table 8.2). Migraine confers no immunity against disease. The primary care physician should not mess with these "worst headaches ever" or "different headaches" in the office. Send them immediately to an Emergency Department where specialized investigations and neurologic consultation are readily available (see Chapter 15, *Emergency Management of Acute Headaches*).

Table 8.2   Red Flags in Migraine Assessment

• Worst headache ever	• Onset with exertion
• Decreased level of awareness	• Meningeal irritation
• Abnormal physical signs (including fever)	• Worsening condition

Treatment of Migraine

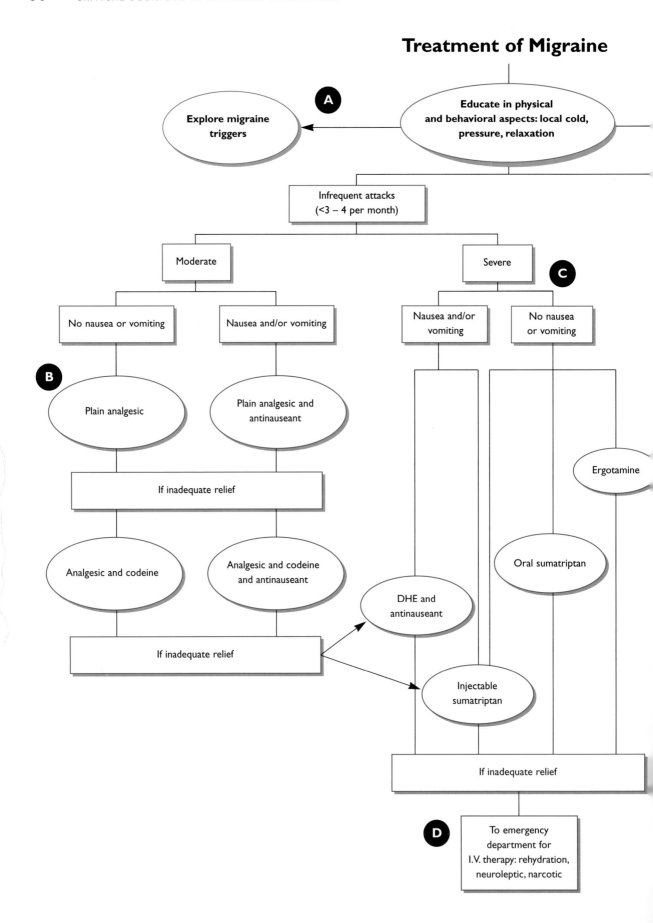

Critical Decisions

(A) Explore migraine triggers / consider headache diary

Triggers
- Psychological: stress release, change in sleep pattern.
- Hormonal: association with menstruation, ovulation, oral contraceptive use, or pregnancy.
- Dietary: reduce red wine, cheese, MSG, aspartame, nuts, chocolate, citrus fruit, diary products.
- Environmental: strong odors, cigarette smoke, barometric pressure change.

Diary
- Record headache frequency, duration, intensity, triggers, treatment used and effectiveness.

(B) Analgesics
- OTCs for mild to moderate.
- Overuse may lead to medication-induced headache (MIH).

(C) Specific antimigraine drugs

Ergotamine
- Must be taken early in attack.
- Avoid use in patients with peripheral vascular disease, increased BP, coronary artery disease.
- May cause nausea and/or vomiting.

Dihydroergotamine (DHE)
- Less nausea and/or vomiting than with ergotamine.
- Less vasoconstriction.
- Routes: IM, SQ, IV, and nasal.

Sumatriptan (Imitrex)
- Similar contraindications as above.
- Routes: PO, SQ, and nasal.
- May cause chest pain.

(D) Treatment of ultrasevere migraine attacks
- IV DHE, narcotics, neuroleptics.

(E) Beta-blockers

Nadolol
- Less penetration of the CNS.
- Less drowsiness and depression.
- Start low and go slow, allow 8 to 12 weeks of treatment before maximum benefit seen.
- Avoid use in patients with asthma or diabetes mellitus.

(F) Calcium channel blockers
- Sibelium 10 mg q.h.s for at least 9 weeks to achieve maximum benefit.
- Avoid use in patients with depression.
- May cause weight gain.
- Contraindicated in patients with low blood pressure or arrhythmia.

(G) Tricyclic antidepressants
- Amitriptyline and doxepin.
- Useful in patients with sleep disturbance.
- Dosage: 50 to 70 mg q.h.s.

(H) Combination therapy
- Tricyclic and beta blocker.
- Tricyclic and calcium channel blocker.
- NOT beta-blocker and calcium channel blocker.

(I) Other medications

Pizotifen
- Dosage: 2 to 5 mg q.h.s
- May cause drowsiness and weight gain.

Valproate
- 1000 to 2000 mg/day

Methysergide
- Powerful medication, requires a 30-day rest period after 6 months of use.
- Side effects are rare, but include fibrosis and vasoconstriction.

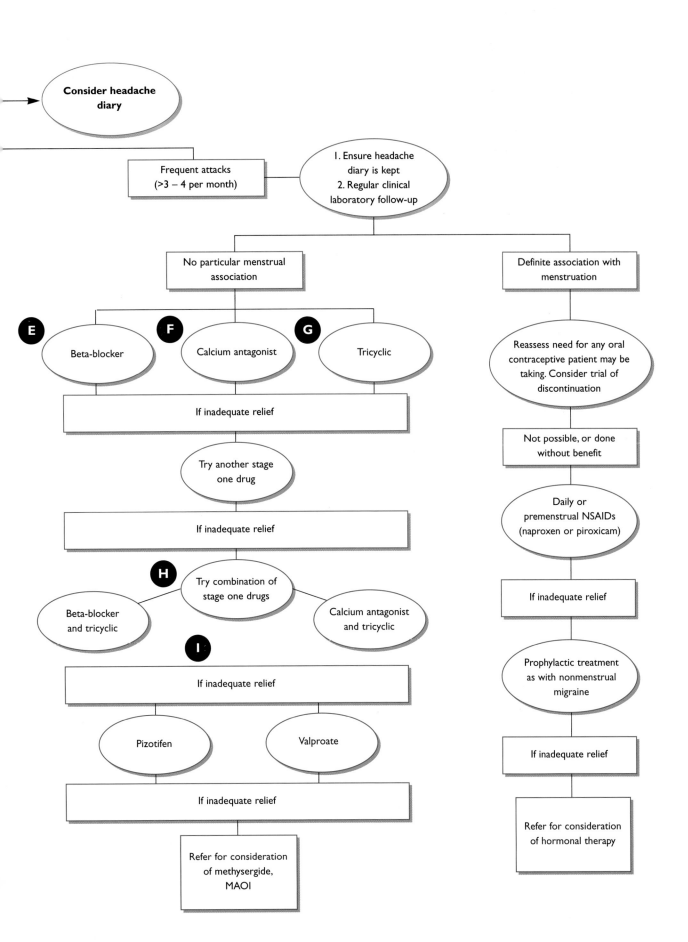

Bibliography

Anthony M. Unilateral migraine or occipital neuralgia? In: Clifford F. ed. New advances in headache research. London: Smith-Gordon Publishers, 1989:39–43.

Anthony M, Lance JW. Monoamine oxidase inhibitors in the treatment of migraine. Arch Neurol 1969; 21:263–268.

Blau JN. Migraine prodromes separated from the aura: complete migraine. BMJ 1980; 281:658–660.

Dahlof C. Placebo-controlled clinical trials with ergotamine in the acute treatment of migraine. Cephalalgia 1993; 13:166–171.

Davidoff RA. Migraine: Manifestations, pathogenesis and management. Contemporary Neurology series, Volume 42. Philadelphia: F.A. Davis Company, 1995:54.

Edmeads J, Grenville A, Aube M. Migraine variability: an underrecognized impediment to effective treatment. Pain Res Manage 1996; 1:215–218.

Edmeads JG. Recent advances in pharmacotherapy: migraine. Can Med Assoc J 1988; 138:107–112.

Edmeads J, Findlay H, Tugwell P, et al. Impact of migraine and tension-type headache on life-style, consulting behaviour and medication use. A Canadian population survey. Can J Neurol Sci 1993; 20:131–137.

Edmeads J. Bringing treatment to a head. Headache 1991; 31:695.

Graham JR. Methysergide for prevention of headache. Experience in five hundred patients over three years. N Engl J Med 1964; 270:67–72.

Green JE. A survey of migraine in England 1975–1976. Headache 1977; 17:67–68.

Hering R, Kuritzky A. Sodium valproate in the prophylactic treatment of migraine: a double-blind study versus placebo. Cephalalgia 1992; 12:81–84.

Hoffert MJ, Couch JR, Diamond S, et al. Transnasal butorphanol in the treatment of acute migraine. Headache 1995; 35:65–69.

Jensen K. Tfelt-Hansen P, Lauritzen M, Olesen J. Classic migraine. A prospective recording of symptoms. Acta Neurol Scand 1986; 73:359–362.

Klapper J, Stanton J. The emergency treatment of acute migraine headache: a comparison of intravenous dihydroergotamine, dexamethasone, and placebo. Cephalalgia 1991; 11 (Suppl 2):159–160.

Linet MS, Stewart WF, Celentano D, et al. An epidemiologic survey of headaches among adolescents and young adults. JAMA 1989; 261:221–226.

Peroutka SJ, Banghart SB, Allen GS. Relative potency and selectivity of calcium antagonists used in the treatment of migraine. Headache 1984; 24:55–58.

Pryse-Phillips W, Findlay F, Tugwell P, et al. A Canadian population survey on the clinical, epidemiologic and societal impact of migraine and tension-type headaches. Can J Neurol Sci 1992; 19:333–339.

Richardson PH, Vincent CA. Acupuncture for the treatment of pain: a review of evaluative research. Pain 1986; 24:15–40.

Robbins L. Precipitating factors in migraine : a retrospective review of 494 patients. Headache 1994; 34:214–216.

Selby G, Lance JW. Observations on 500 cases of migraine and allied vascular headache. J Neurol Neurosurg Psychiatry 1960; 22:23–32.

Solomon S. OTC analgesics in treating common primary headaches: a review of safety and efficacy. Headache 1994; 34(Suppl 1):13–21.

Stewart WF, Lipton RB, Celentano DD, Reed ML. Prevalence of migraine headache in the United States. Relation to age, income, race and other sociodemographic factors. JAMA 1992; 267:64–69.

Tfelt-Hansen P, Standness B, Kangasniemi P, et al. Timolol vs propranolol vs placebo in common migraine prophylaxis: a double-blind multicentre trial. Acta Neurol Scand 1984; 69:1–8.

The Dihydroergotamine Nasal Spray Multicenter Investigators. Efficacy, safety, and tolerability of dihydroergotamine nasal spray as monotherapy in the treatment of acute migraine. Headache 1995; 35:177–184.

The Subcutaneous Sumatriptan International Study Group. Treatment of migraine attacks with sumatriptan. N Engl J Med 1991; 325:316–321.

Weisz MA, El-Raheb M, Blumenthal HJ. Home administration of intramuscular DHE for the treatment of acute migraine headache. Headache 1994; 34:371–373.

Whitty CWM, Hokaday JM, Whitty MM. The effect of oral contraceptives on migraine. BMJ 1980; 281:658–660.

Ziegler DK, Hurwitz A, Hassanein RS, et al. Migraine prophylaxis. A comparison of propranolol and amitriptyline. Arch Neurol 1987; 44:486–489.

Supplementary Search Strategies

SuSS 1

Subject	Headache (index term)
Subject	Drug Therapy (subheading)
Limited to	Human
AND	Meta-Analysis (publication type) or Clinical Trial (publication type)
AND	1994 through 1997

SuSS 2

Subject	Migraine (index term)
Subject	Medical History Taking+(index term) or explode Physical Examination (index term) or explode Sensitivity and Specificity+ (index term)
Limited to	Human
AND	1994 through 1997

SuSS 3	
Subject	Migraine (index term)
Subject	explode Therapy (subheading)
Limited to	Human
AND	Meta-Analysis (publication type) or Clinical Trial (publication type)
AND	1994 through 1997

Chapter 9

CLUSTER HEADACHE

DIAGNOSIS

Cluster headache is among the most severe pain conditions. The stereotyped pattern of the attacks and the intensity of pain allow the diagnosis of cluster headaches to be made on history alone.

These headaches cluster in time, typically. One or more (usually two or three) brief attacks occur every day, for months at a time, and then cease, remaining absent for months or years—only to recur in another month(s)-long cluster.

The International Headache Society classifies cluster headache into episodic and chronic varieties. Episodic cluster occurs as noted. Chronic cluster, by definition, occurs when there is a complete absence of remission. Chronic cluster is subdivided into chronic unremitting from the onset, and chronic cluster evolving from episodic cluster.

The clinical presentation of cluster is quite typical. Unlike migraine, it predominantly affects males in a 8:1 ratio to females. Onset is usually over the age of 20, but it may occur at any age. There may be some periodicity to the attacks; a seasonal component with occurrence in spring and autumn seems to be a pattern. Clusters typically last 2 to 3 months and occur on a yearly basis, though longer remissions, lasting up to 2 years at a time, are common.

Typically, the pain of an attack peaks within 10 to 15 minutes and lasts 45 to 60 minutes, but it may continue up to 2 to 3 hours. The attack frequency usually is between 1 and 3 times in a day. The pain may be provoked by alcohol but more often is spontaneous. Patients describe the pain as penetrating, excruciating, and occurring in the retroorbital temporal region. Frequently these patients may hold their head in their hands, pacing, or rocking backward and forward. They are often unable to sit or lie still for any period of time during the attack.

Attacks are nocturnal in a large percentage of patients, are unilateral, always on the same side in any one cluster, and may be accompanied by lacrimation, unilateral conjunctival injection, rhinorrhea, ptosis, or miosis (Figure 9.1).

On physical examination, these patients may have ipsilateral scalp, face, or carotid artery tenderness in addition to the autonomic findings. A typical leonine facial appearance characterizes many individuals with cluster headache (Figure 9.2). This appearance is associated with deep facial furrows, forehead creases, ruddy complexion, nasal telangiectasia, and broad chin. The figure illustrates the derivation of the term.

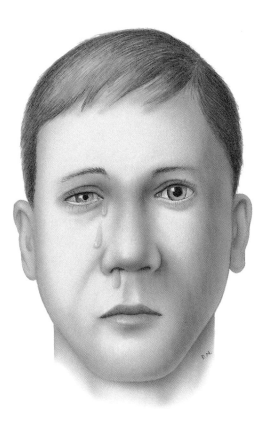

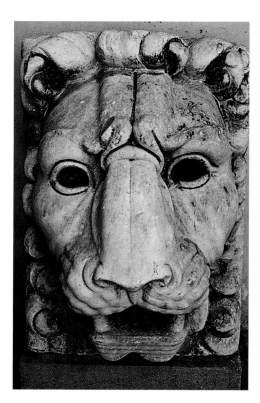

Figure 9.1   Typical findings associated with acute attacks of cluster headache, including unilateral lacrimation, conjunctival injection, rhinorrhea, ptosis, or miosis.

Figure 9.2   Wall plaque (16th century) in Italy illustrating the large, coarse, creased features

DIFFERENTIAL DIAGNOSIS

Although the history of a cluster headache is quite typical, various other possibilities should be considered in the differential diagnosis. *Migraine* may present in a similar pattern as cluster; however, the attacks of cluster are shorter lived, are always unilateral, often nocturnal, occur up to several times a day, and usually are not associated with nausea or vomiting.

Temporal arteritis pain is associated with a waxing/waning quality. Frequently it is associated with polymyalgia rheumatica, and the pain may be exacerbated by chewing. In *trigeminal neuralgia,* the brief jabs of pain may last seconds at a time. Jabs are described as an electric lancinating pain, frequently triggered by simply touching, chewing, or yawning. Usually, trigeminal neuralgia involves the V_2 and V_3 areas of the face; V_1 involvement is extremely rare.

Pericarotid syndrome has a similar clinical presentation to cluster including unilateral severe pain with autonomic features; however, the pain is usually more persistent, initially severe at the onset, with gradually reducing intensity. Typically, it is associated with Horner's syndrome and a trigeminal sensory loss. A word of caution in diagnosing pericarotid syndrome: be careful to exclude carotid occlusion, dissection, or aneurysm. These conditions may be life-threatening and are potentially reversible. Carotid ultrasound and angiography should be considered when they are suspected. The pericarotid syndrome, more likely than not, is associated with a lesion, such as aneurysm or tumor.

Indomethacin-responsive headache syndromes represent a unique group of primary headache disorders which are characterized by a prompt, absolute, and often permanent response to indomethacin. These headache disorders are more common than previously appreciated, but are often overlooked in clinical practice, even by neurologists. This is unfortunate since these patients suffer unnecessarily for years when a quick solution for the patient and a gratifying clinical experience for the physician could have been achieved through proper therapy. Indomethacin-responsive headache disorders can be easily confused with cluster headache because of the accompanying autonomic features associated with individual headaches. Cluster headaches, however, can be distinguished by their sex prediliction, being a predominantly male disorder. Indomethacin-responsive paroxysmal hemicranias can also be distinguished from cluster headache by their short duration and high frequency of attacks. (Table 9.1)

Table 9.1   Clinical Features of Cluster Variants

Sex F:M	CPH 3:1	EPH 1:1	SUNCT 1:8	HC 1.8:1	Hypnic 1.7:1	Cluster 1:9
Pain quality	Stabbing, pulsatile, boring	Stabbing, pulsatile, boring	Stabbing, lancinating	Baseline dull ache superimposed throbbing/stabbing	Throbbing	Stabbing boring
Pain severity	Very severe	Very severe	Moderate	Moderate to severe	Moderate	Very severe
Site of maximal pain	Orbit Temple	Orbit Temple	Periorbital	Orbit Temple	Generalized	Orbit Temple
Attacks per day	1–40	3–30	1/day–1/30-hr	Variable	1–3/night	0–8
Attack duration	2–45 min	1–30 min	15–20 sec	Minutes to days	15–30 min	15–180 min
Autonomic features	Present	Present	Present	Present (but less pronounced than cluster)	Absent	Present
Alcohol triggers attacks	Yes	Yes	Yes	No	No	Yes
Nocturnal attacks	Yes	Yes	Yes	Yes	Yes	Yes
Indomethacin response	Absolute	Absolute	No	Absolute	No	Variable

CPH: Chronic Paroxysmal Hemicrania; EPH: Episodic Paroxysmal Hemicrania; SUNCT: Short-lasting, Unilateral, Neuralgiform headache attacks with Conjunctival injection, Tearing, rhinorrhea and forehead sweating.

Chronic paroxysmal hemicrania and episodic paroxysmal hemicrania differ mainly in their temporal profile. The latter, as the name implies, is characterized by discrete attacks and remission phases. The headache phase can range from 1 week to 5 months, whereas remission periods range from 1 to 36 months. Both chronic and episodic paroxysmal hemicranias manifest as frequent and daily attacks of severe, short-lived, unilateral, orbital, suborbital, or temporal pain lasting approximately 20 minutes (range 2 to 45 minutes). There is at least one ipsilateral autonomic feature which may include lacrimation, ptosis, eyelid edema, conjunctival injection, nasal congestion or rhinorrea.

Hemicrania continua is a continuous unilateral pain in the head which may involve the entire hemicranium or occasionally be confined to a focal region. The continuous headache is punctuated by painful unilateral exacerbations lasting 20 minutes to several days. These periods of heightened intensity of pain are often accompanied by one or more autonomic features as well as idiopathic stabbing headaches (ice-pick headaches). It is important to bear in mind that this headache disorder may sometimes resemble a prolonged unilateral migraine attack lasting several days to weeks, with headache-free remissions. In fact, it is our opinion that any nonorganic unilateral headache which does not respond to conventional migraine agents, particularily if autonomic features are present, deserves a short trial of indomethacin.

A caveat to bear in mind when confronted with a patient with any one of these headache syndromes, is that *all* patients, despite the presence of classic clinical characteristics, require neuroimaging to exclude a structural cause since organic mimicks have been described.

In addition to these peculiar hemicranias, a group of "situational headaches" may also respond to indomethacin. These include *brief* headaches that are triggered by cough, or a similar brief Valsalva maneuver (lifting, straining, sneezing); gradual headaches precipitated by sustained exertion; and headaches brought on by sexual intercourse. Extreme caution must be exercised in these groups of patients, and neuroimaging is required to exclude a structural mass, posterior fossa abnormality, or subarachnoid hemorrage.

Although treatment is often not required in patients with ice-pick headache because the jabs of pain are brief, the attacks can sometimes occur with an unacceptable frequency. In such cases, treatment with indomethacin often produces a prompt and persistent response.

Indomethacin is effective in dosages ranging from 25 to 250 mg daily. The usual starting dose is 25 mg thrice daily with meals. The dosage is titrated based on the patients response and side-effect profile. A slow-release preparation or rectal suppository is available for patients with nocturnal breakthough headaches, and for those with gastric intolerance. A treatment response is usually seen within 48 hours. Tachyphylaxis is not seen, but withdrawal from medication will usually be met with recurrence of the headaches. The treatment, therefore, can be said to provide long-term relief, not a cure.

TREATMENT

As always, patient education is the initial step in treatment of cluster headache. Patients should understand the condition in terms of its behavior, including its exacerbation by alcohol. They need reassurance that there is no underlying lesion causing their pain.

Medical management can be divided into abortive treatment of the individual attacks, and prophylactic management of the cluster. Prophylactic medication is the treatment of choice in most cases since the acute attacks are so short-lived that the abortive measures frequently do not have time to be effective.

Oxygen inhalation by mask at about 7 liters per minute shortens the duration of individual headaches about 70% of the time; nobody knows why.

Subcutaneous *sumatriptan* in doses of 6 mg has been shown to be effective within 5 minutes of administration. In view of the slower onset of action, the oral route is not the route of choice; however, intranasal sumatriptan may be used in this situation and is available in a 20mg dose. Contraindications for *sumatriptan* [Imitrex] include a history of hypertension, peripheral vascular disease, myocardial infarction disease or angina, and concurrent use of other 5-HT$_1$ agonist medications (see Chapter 8, *Treatment of Migraine*).

Ergotamine tartrate may be taken sublingually, 2 mg at the onset of the headache, repeated in a half hour to a maximum of three doses in a 24-hour period. However, the attack may subside spontaneously before the drug becomes effective and therefore the sublingual route is not preferred.

Dihydroergotamine (DHE) may be given subcutaneously, intramuscularly, or intravenously. The route of administration may limit its use in some situations. The dosage is 0.5 to 1 mg, using any of the above routes, repeated in 1 hour as needed. This may be better tolerated when combined with an antinausea agent such as Maxeran 10 mg. Intranasal DHE has recently been marketed for migraine; its rapid onset of action may make it one of the treatments of choice for attacks of cluster headache.

If the attacks are predictable, then oral or sublingual *ergotamine* may be tried 30 to 60 minutes before an expected attack, particularly if the attacks are nocturnal in their onset. Maximum dosage of ergotamine is 3 to 4 mg daily, for short (maximum 1 or 2 weeks) periods of time.

Prevention is the preferred management. A number of drugs have been shown to be effective.

Calcium channel blockers may take weeks to achieve efficacy, which may limit their use in cluster headache; however, their use may be indicated in situations where clusters last several months. Verapamil in doses of 80 mg q.i.d. or Verapamil SR 240 mg per day, is helpful. Similarly, Sibelium (Flunarizine) 10 mg h.s. may be used under similar circumstances.

Lithium carbonate is an effective treatment for episodic and chronic cluster headache. The dosage is 300 mg t.i.d. with levels monitored daily until stabilized (0.8–1.2 mEq/L). Follow-up of lithium levels biweekly should be done to monitor for potential toxicity. Side effects include tremor, gastrointestinal discomfort, and lethargy. Close monitoring of BUN and serum creatinine levels and urinalysis are advised for evidence of nephrotoxicity. Thyroid function should also be checked every 3 to 6 months. Diuretics and low salt diets should be avoided, since low sodium may elevate lithium levels.

Sansert (methysergide) is a very effective medication in the treatment of chronic cluster headaches. Daily dosage should be started at 2 mg (one tablet), gradually increasing over the course of 5 to 6 days to a maximum of 3 to 4 tablets per day. Side effects include nausea, dizziness, leg cramps and gastrointestinal discomfort. Although rare (1/1500), the most serious side effect of Sansert is retroperitoneal fibrosis. Therefore, it is recommended that a patient taking Sansert discontinue the medication after a six-month interval for at least a month, since fibrotic complications are usually reversible. (This limitation makes Sansert unsatisfactory for long-term use in chronic cluster headache.) Coronary artery disease, hypertension, peripheral vascular disease, phlebitis, collagen vascular disease, compromised liver or renal function, and pregnancy are contraindications to its use.

Prednisone in the usual dosage of 40 to 80 mg daily for 5 to 7 days may be started, gradually tapering the dosage after this time at a point when the patient becomes comfortable. The usual contraindications to the use of steroids apply. Prednisone is not indicated for long-term use, but (like Sansert) can be used to knock headaches down quickly until the slower-acting agents, such as verapamil, valproate, and lithium, can begin to work.

Although the mechanism of action of *valproic acid* is not well understood, it has been shown to be effective in prevention of cluster attacks in certain cases. Dosage is 250 mg t.i.d. initially, with increasing dosages as tolerated to 500 mg q.i.d. if necessary. Side effects may include weight gain, gastric discomfort, thrombocytopenia, tremor, and transient hair loss.

Surgical management may be indicated for attacks of pain that are chronic (persisting more than a year) without remissions, or with remissions lasting less than 14 days. Magnetic resonance imaging is required to exclude the possibility of an underlying structural lesion. Surgery should only be considered if maximal medical management has failed. A variety of surgical procedures can be tried: the general principle is either ablation of components of the trigeminal nerve or autonomic pathway (nervus intermedius). The most effective surgical treatment is trigeminal gangliorhizolysis—which works only in about 50% of cases.

Critical Decisions

A Abortive treatment
• Patient education re: exacerbating factors (i.e., alcohol), and reassurance of no underlying lesion.

B Acute attacks
• Pain peaks within 10–15 minutes, lasting 45–60 minutes.
• Attack frequency: 1–3 times per day.
• Pain is penetrating, excruciating and retroorbital.
• Attacks may be nocturnal.

C Prophylaxis
• Prophylaxis is indicated in every case.

D Drug therapy
• Advantages of Imitrex® (sumatriptan): rapid onset of action; routes of administration include SQ and intranasal.
• Contraindications include hypertension, peripheral vascular disease, coronary artery disease, and use of various other medications (see Chapter 8, *Migraine*).

E DHE treatment
• Advantage of DHE: wide variety of routes of administration, including , IM, SQ, and intranasal.
• May need to be combined with antiemetic agent (Maxeran®) for improved tolerability.

F Surgery
• Indicated when medical approach ineffective.
• Surgical methods include percutaneous radiofrequency trigeminal gangliorhizolysis and posterior fossa trigeminal sensory rhizotomy with section of nervus intermedius.

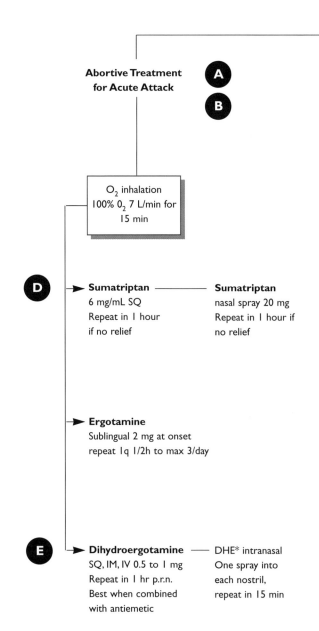

Abortive Treatment for Acute Attack A B

O_2 inhalation 100% O_2 7 L/min for 15 min

D **Sumatriptan** 6 mg/mL SQ Repeat in 1 hour if no relief — **Sumatriptan** nasal spray 20 mg Repeat in 1 hour if no relief

Ergotamine Sublingual 2 mg at onset repeat 1q 1/2h to max 3/day

E **Dihydroergotamine** SQ, IM, IV 0.5 to 1 mg Repeat in 1 hr p.r.n. Best when combined with antiemetic — DHE* intranasal One spray into each nostril, repeat in 15 min

Treatment of Cluster Headache

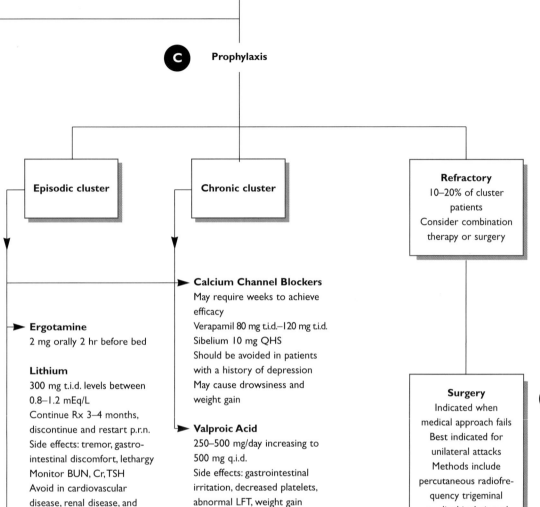

C Prophylaxis

Episodic cluster

Chronic cluster

Refractory
10–20% of cluster patients
Consider combination therapy or surgery

Ergotamine
2 mg orally 2 hr before bed

Lithium
300 mg t.i.d. levels between 0.8–1.2 mEq/L
Continue Rx 3–4 months, discontinue and restart p.r.n.
Side effects: tremor, gastro-intestinal discomfort, lethargy
Monitor BUN, Cr, TSH
Avoid in cardiovascular disease, renal disease, and pregnancy

Sansert
2 mg t.i.d.
Must stop every 6 mo for at least 30 days. Avoid use in cardiovascular, renal and hepatic disease, and in pregnancy

Corticosteroids
40–80 mg/day for 5 days, tapering doses, and discontinue 4–6 weeks
Monitor for well known side effects
Not to be used for chronic cluster
Avoid use in patients with increased blood pressure, diabetes mellitus, peptic ulcer, systemic infection

Calcium Channel Blockers
May require weeks to achieve efficacy
Verapamil 80 mg t.i.d.–120 mg t.i.d.
Sibelium 10 mg QHS
Should be avoided in patients with a history of depression
May cause drowsiness and weight gain

Valproic Acid
250–500 mg/day increasing to 500 mg q.i.d.
Side effects: gastrointestinal irritation, decreased platelets, abnormal LFT, weight gain

Surgery
Indicated when medical approach fails
Best indicated for unilateral attacks
Methods include percutaneous radiofre-quency trigeminal gangliorhizolysis and posterior fossa trigeminal sensory rhizotomy

F

Bibliography

Campbell JK, Onofrio BM. Surgical management of cluster headache. In: Tollison CD, Kunkel RS, eds. Headache diagnosis and treatment. Baltimore: Williams & Wilkins, 1993:205–210.

Ekbom K, Cole JA. Subcutaneous sumatriptan in the acute treatment of cluster headache attacks. Can J Neurol Sci 1993; 20 (Suppl 4): F61.

Ekbom K, Sakai F. Management. In: Olesen J, ed. The headaches. New York: Raven Press, 1993:591–599.

Ekbom K. Treatment of cluster headache: clinical trials, design and results. Cephalalgia 1995 (Suppl 15); 33–36.

Kudrow L. Diagnoses and treatment of cluster headache. Med Clin North Am 1991; 75: 579–594.

Mathew N. Cluster headache. Neurology March 1992; 42 (Suppl 12): 22–31.

Supplementary Search Strategies

SuSS 1	
Subject	Cluster headache (index term)
Subject	explode Diagnosis (subheading)
Limited to	1994 through 1997

SuSS 2	
Subject	Cluster headache (index term)
Subject	explode Therapy or Drug therapy (subheading)
Limited to	1994 through 1997

Chapter 10

HEADACHES ASSOCIATED WITH SPACE-OCCUPYING LESIONS

Brain tumor is an inevitable fear of headache patients and their physicians. In fact, it is the exception that a patient with headache *alone* will harbor a space-occupying lesion. The routine use of neuroimaging is unwarranted in adult patients with clear-cut migraine and no focal signs or symptoms, seizures, or recent change in headache pattern. While the yield may be slightly higher in nonmigrainous headaches, the indiscriminate use of CT/MRI in these patients is not cost-effective, particularly in the era of managed care. This chapter will review the prevalence and characteristics of the headaches in patients with space-occupying lesions and the features which should alert the clinician to the need for special investigations.

HEADACHE AS A SYMPTOM OF SPACE OCCUPATION

Modern neuroimaging has caused a decline in the incidence of headache in brain tumor patients by allowing early detection before lesions grow to a size sufficient to cause headache. Recent studies indicate a headache incidence of about 50% in these patients. However, only one-third are imaged primarily because of headache, and in less than 10% is headache present in isolation. Similar trends of declining incidence have been found for papilledema (10%), exacerbation with Valsalva, and vomiting—previously considered to be defining features of brain tumor headaches.

Headache as a presenting or major feature of a space-occupying lesion is dependent on both the nature and location of the mass. The faster growing, more malignant varieties of brain tumor cause headaches in approximately 50% of patients, whereas slower growing, low-grade supratentorial neoplasms are less likely to cause headache (5%). These tumors more often declare themselves with seizures. Analogous to rapidly evolving brain tumors, subdural hematomas and brain abscesses are more frequently associated with headache (70–90%) as an early and prominent symptom.

Lesion *location* is an equally if not a more important determinant for headache development than lesion *type,* especially with respect to brain tumors. Posterior fossa (infratentorial) lesions are more commonly associated with headache and other classical brain tumor features (vomiting, papilledema, worsening with Valsalva), likely because of CSF pathway obstruction which leads to an early rise in intracranial pressure. This is illustrated in the higher prevalence of headache in pediatric brain tumor populations (70%) where infratentorial tumors account for approximately 50% of primary brain neoplasms in children of all ages. In addition, because of the density of eloquent neurologic structures confined in such close proximity, headaches quickly become associated with demonstrable neurologic abnormalities. Not surprisingly then, high grade neoplasms situated in the posterior fossa announce themselves early with headache.

PATHOPHYSIOLOGY

Space-occupying lesions cause headache by distorting, compressing, or by causing traction on pain-sensitive intracranial structures (Figure 10.1). The proposed mechanism of headache involves either local traction on pain-sensitive structures or distant traction by mass effect or hydrocephalus. The brain parenchyma is not sensitive to pain, and raised intracranial pressure alone is felt to be insufficient to cause headache.

Like any visceral pain, pain arising from the intracranial cavity is referred to superficial areas which share innervation with the structures involved. Although the localizing value of dural-based pain is controversial, in general, lateralized lesions which initially cause local traction refer pain ipsilaterally, supratentorial lesions refer pain to the frontal region, and posterior fossa lesions refer pain to the ear, or to the lower occiput and upper cervical region. As intracranial pressure rises, a mass lesion may cause distant traction by distorting more remote pain-sensitive structures, thereby referring pain to a site distant from the lesion.

Less commonly, carcinomatous meningitis may cause a generalized headache due to diffuse leptomeningeal involvement and, although exceedingly rare, brain tumors may mimic migraine, even with a visual aura. Migrainous headaches with focal neurologic symptoms have been also described in children treated successfully (by radiation) for posterior fossa and pineal tumors in the absence of tumor recurrence.

Colloid cyst in
3rd ventricle

Subdural
hematoma

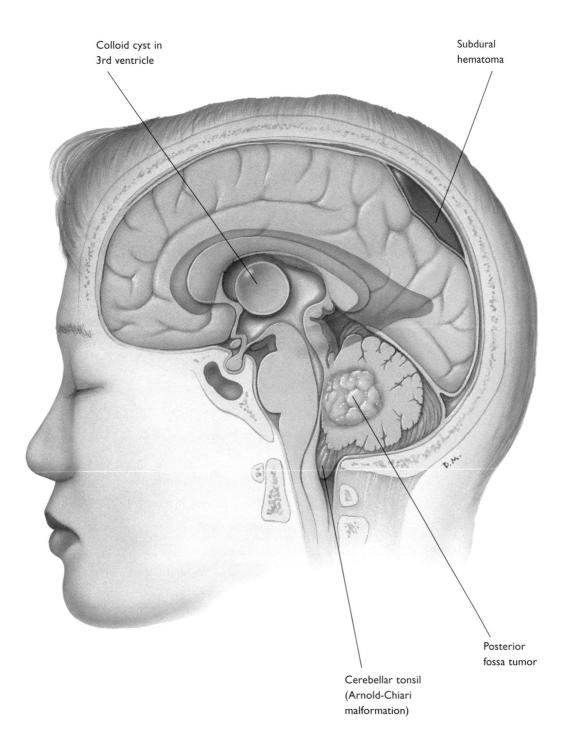

Posterior
fossa tumor

Cerebellar tonsil
(Arnold-Chiari
malformation)

Figure 10.1   Space-occupying lesions cause headache by distorting or compressing pain-sensitive structures or by causing CSF outflow obstruction, thereby raising intracranial pressure.

HEADACHE CHARACTERISTICS IN PATIENTS WITH MASS LESIONS

Coincident with the decline in headache as an early, major, and isolated feature of brain tumors, earlier detection has led to the diminishing number of "classic brain tumor headache" presentations which we as clinicians have been taught to recognize.

Headache Type and Severity

Space-occupying headaches are typically subacute in duration and progressive in nature. The most common types of headache in brain tumor patients are dull, aching, pressure or "sinus-like" headaches which closely mimic tension-type headaches. The pain intensity is moderate to severe, but in a significant minority is initially described as mild. These headaches are usually intermittent, at least initially, often lasting for several hours in duration. This type of headache is present in about 75% of patients who have headaches, with the remaining headaches either resembling migraine, or being nondescript and unclassifiable. Space-occupying lesions rarely present as migraine, however in the absence of atypical symptoms or abnormal physical signs (Table 10.1).

The headache associated with rapidly evolving space-occupying lesions such as subdural or epidural hematomas, and brain abscesses, are typically more intense, persistent, and less likely to resolve with simple analgesics.

Two distinctive types of headache deserve special attention. *Intermittent, sudden, paroxysmal headaches* typically precipitated by changes in posture, and occasionally associated with sudden leg weakness (drop attacks), vertigo, visual blurring, loss of consciousness or sudden death may be seen with "benign" intra-ventricular lesions. The classic example is a colloid cyst of the third ventricle. The mechanism is felt to be either intermittent ventricular obstruction ("ball-valve" effect) or sudden rises in intracranial pressure ("plateau waves") superimposed on a state of chronic mild increased intracranial pressure.

The second unique headache syndrome is *cough or exertional headache.* This is a characteristically benign headache syndrome manifested by sudden, brief, severe head pains precipitated by coughing or other maneuvers which raise intracranial pressure. However, intracranial masses or structural abnormalities may be present in 2 to 11% of this population. Therefore, *all* patients with this headache syndrome should be imaged with MRI.

Headache Location

As a general rule, space-occupying headaches have poor localizing value except when unilateral. Bifrontal headaches are most common in patients with space-occupying lesions, particularly when associated with increased intracranial pressure. Neck pain and occipital headache are often seen when intracranial pressure is raised whether the mass is supra- or infratentorial. Again, this headache pattern is more typical with rapidly expanding lesions that cause an early rise in intracranial pressure; however, careful questioning may elicit a history of an earlier or initially unilateral headache caused by local traction, before the rise in intracranial pressure caused distant traction and deceptive or nonlocalizing patterns of pain referral.

Associated Signs and Symptoms

Nausea, vomiting, and resistance to analgesics as associated headache symptoms are present in 50% of brain tumor patients. These features should signal organicity and the need for investigation, unless associated with clear-cut migraine. Other neurologic features such as weakness, seizures, and confusion are present in the majority of cases.

The classical triggers or exacerbators for space-occupying headache (head movement, bending, straining, coughing, and sudden changes in posture), are non-specific and present in only 25% of patients.

Table 10.1   Common Clinical Features of Space-occupying Headache

Nondescript bifrontal headaches	Headache is rare in isolation without one or
Headache character resembles tension-type	more of the following features:
or "sinus" headache	Nausea and/or vomiting
Headache profile is subacute and progressive	Confusion
Moderate to severe intensity	Seizures
Resistance to analgesics	Weakness
More often associated with malignant or	Aggravation with changes in position
rapidly evolving masses	Abnormal neurologic signs
Early headache presentation with	
posterior fossa lesions	

Critical Decisions

A **Headache with systemic symptoms**
- May indicate underlying infection, inflammatory/autoimmune disorder or malignancy.
- General nonspecific symptoms include sweats, chills, malaise, fatigue, anorexia, myalgias, and weight loss.
- Underlying infectious illness is suggested by presence of fever, cough, dysuria, and leukocytosis.

B **Meningeal irritation/increased intracranial pressure**
- Meningismus, photophobia, irritability, cranial nerve palsies, and radicular symptoms usually signify a meningeal process.
- Meningeal signs may be subtle or absent in the very young and old, and in those who are immunocompromised or comatose.
- Meningeal signs are often accompanied by signs suggestive of increased intracranial pressure, such as vomiting, papilledema, lethargy, confusion, or decreased level of consciousness.

C **Lumbar puncture**
- Should be done in any patient with a subacute headache when a meningeal process is suspected.
- Recommended that patients be tapped and treated for presumed infection prior to lab confirmation in absence of focal neurologic findings.
- Management is based on the most likely organism.
- Purulent bacterial meningitis is often associated with brisk neutrophilic pleocytosis, hypoglycorrachia (CSF/serum glucose < 0.30, usually < 0.21), and an elevated CSF protein.

- Encephalitis has a similar CSF profile, but quantitatively less dramatic and the pleocytosis is usually lymphocytic predominant. Glucose is usually normal.
- In neoplastic meningitis, the pleocytosis is usually less robust, lymphocytic, and often associated with atypical cells. The CSF glucose may be significantly reduced (0.3) and the protein is elevated similar to bacterial meningitis.
- Aseptic meningitis has a characteristic lymphocytic pleocytosis associated with a normal or only slightly aberrant protein or glucose concentration.

D **Intracranial involvement**
- Headache and systemic symptoms associated with seizures, confusion, stroke or stroke-like episodes (particularly when CT is normal) should raise possibility of a CNS vasculitis.
- CNS vasculitis may occur in the setting of a systemic vasculitis or as an isolated vasculitis confined to the CNS.

E **MRI**
- In cases of CNS vasculitis, MRI will reveal multifocal areas of increased T2-weighted signal throughout the cerebral white and possibly gray matter.
- Catheter angiography is the gold standard for diagnosis, but tissue biopsy may be required because of a 20% false-negative angiographic rate.
- MRI with contrast may be valuable in patients with leptomeningeal malignancies and in patients with herpes and other parenchymal encephalitides.

Sinister Headaches

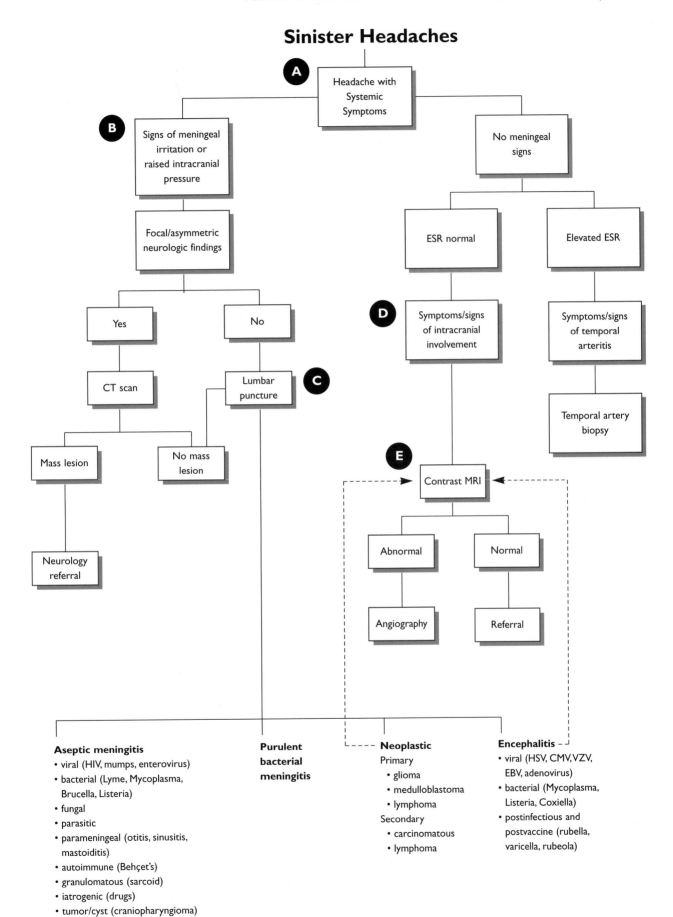

A Headache with Systemic Symptoms

B Signs of meningeal irritation or raised intracranial pressure

No meningeal signs

Focal/asymmetric neurologic findings

ESR normal

Elevated ESR

Yes

No

D Symptoms/signs of intracranial involvement

Symptoms/signs of temporal arteritis

CT scan

Lumbar puncture **C**

Temporal artery biopsy

Mass lesion

No mass lesion

E Contrast MRI

Neurology referral

Abnormal

Normal

Angiography

Referral

Aseptic meningitis
- viral (HIV, mumps, enterovirus)
- bacterial (Lyme, Mycoplasma, Brucella, Listeria)
- fungal
- parasitic
- parameningeal (otitis, sinusitis, mastoiditis)
- autoimmune (Behçet's)
- granulomatous (sarcoid)
- iatrogenic (drugs)
- tumor/cyst (craniopharyngioma)

Purulent bacterial meningitis

Neoplastic
Primary
- glioma
- medulloblastoma
- lymphoma
Secondary
- carcinomatous
- lymphoma

Encephalitis
- viral (HSV, CMV, VZV, EBV, adenovirus)
- bacterial (Mycoplasma, Listeria, Coxiella)
- postinfectious and postvaccine (rubella, varicella, rubeola)

RECOGNIZING THE SINISTER HEADACHE

Because the "classic brain tumor" headache is uncommon, and most space-occupying headaches resemble tension-type headaches and often retain the same character as an individual's previous headaches, the importance of an acute clinical awareness, a thorough headache history, and a careful neurologic examination cannot be overstated. The judicious and appropriate use of neuroimaging in this context is therefore guided by attention to the following "warning signals":

- Subacute or progressive headache over days to months
- Headache with nausea or vomiting not explained by migraine (IHS defined), or systemic illness
- Headaches associated with nocturnal occurrence or morning awakening
- Headaches precipitated or exacerbated by Valsalva maneuvers or sudden changes in position or posture
- New onset in adult life (>40 years) or a *change* in an established headache pattern including increased frequency or intensity, refractoriness to medication, or the acquisition of new features
- Any headache associated with neurologic symptoms (confusion, weakness, etc.) or abnormal physical sign on neurologic examination

These features appear self-evident and may be redundant, but this is intentional. They should be committed to memory and consciously appraised in each patient presenting with headache. The presence of any of these potentially sinister features should prompt immediate referral and neuroimaging.

Bibliography

Alter M, Daube JR, Franklin G, et al. Practice parameter: the utility of neuroimaging in the evaluation of patients with normal neurological examinations. Neurology 1994; 44:1353–1354.

Britt RH. Brain abscess. In: Wilkins RH, Rengachary SS, eds. Neurosurgery. New York: McGraw-Hill, 1985:1928–1956.

Dalessio DJ. Clinical observations on headache. In: Dalessio DJ, ed. Wolff's headache and other head pain (5th ed.). New York: Oxford University Press, 1987:407–422.

Dumas MD, Pexman JHW, Kreeft JH. Computed tomography evaluation of patients with chronic headache. Can Med Assoc J 1994; 151:1447–1452.

Forsythe PA, Posner JB. Headaches in patients with brain tumors. A study of 111 patients. Neurology 1993; 43:1678–1683.

Frishberg BM. The utility of neuroimaging in the evaluation of headache in patients with normal neurological examinations. (Views and Reviews). Neurology 1994; 44:1191–1197.

Iversen HK, Strange P, Sommer W, Tyalve E. Brain tumor headache related to tumor size, histology and location. Cephalalgia 1987; 7(Suppl 6):394–395.

Kennedy CR, Nathwani A. Headache as a presenting feature of brain tumors in children. Cephalalgia 1995; 15(Suppl 16):15.

Lavyne MH, Patterson RH. Headache associated with brain tumor. In: Dalessio DJ, ed. Wolff's headache and other head pain (5th ed.). New York: Oxford University Press, 1987:343–351.

McKissock W. Subdural hematoma. A review of 389 cases. Lancet 1960; 1:1365–1370.

Rooke ED. Benign exertional headache. Med Clin North Am 1968; 52:801–808.

Schlake HP, Grotemeyer KH, Husstedt IW, et al. Symptomatic migraine: intracranial lesions mimicking migrainous headache—a report of three cases. Headache 1991; 31:661–665.

Shuper A, Packer RJ, Vezina LG, et al. Complicated migraine-like episodes in children following cranial irradiation and chemotherapy. Neurology 1995; 45:1837–1840.

Symonds C. Cough headache. Brain 1956; 79:557–568.

Vasquez-Barquero A, Ibanez FJ, Herrera S, et al. Isolated headache as the presenting clinical manifestation of intracranial tumor: a prospective study. Cephalalgia 1994; 14:270–272.

Supplementary Search Strategy

SuSS 1	
Subject	Headache+ (index term)
Subject	explode Brain Neoplasms (index term) or tumor (text word)
	or tumour (text word)
Limited to	1994 through 1997

Chapter 11

INFLAMMATORY HEADACHES

Headache is a frequent symptom of inflammation involving pain-sensitive intra- and extracranial structures. Involvement of these structures may occur in the setting of either localized pathology or disseminated systemic disease or infection.

CRANIAL VASCULITIS

Giant cell arteritis (GCA), also known as temporal arteritis or cranial arteritis, is a systemic inflammatory disease with protean manifestations. Although headache is a major feature in more than 90% of cases, the variability in location, severity, and temporal profile necessitates an index of suspicion which often rests on the following associated features:

- Age of onset older than 50 years.
- New-onset, localized, progressive headache.
- Local symptoms (superficial temporal artery swelling, erythema, tenderness, and pulselessness).
- Cranial symptoms (scalp tenderness, jaw claudication, and pain in the throat, neck, teeth, gums, or eye).
- Neurologic symptoms (transient visual obscurations, diplopia, mental sluggishness, and, in rare cases, stroke).
- Systemic symptoms (fever, weight loss, anorexia, malaise, myalgias, sweating, and chills).
- Elevated erythrocyte sedimentation rate (ESR>40).
- Elevated acute phase reactants (C-reactive protein, von Willebrand's factor, fibrinogen, platelets, lymphocytes, immunoglobulins).

Temporal artery biopsy should proceed in any patient over the age of 50 with a new onset headache when a clinical suspicion of cranial arteritis exists. If vision is threatened, immediate treatment with 40 to 60 mg of prednisone should commence prior to biopsy. Since "skip lesions" is a histologic hallmark, a bilateral biopsy may be necessary, with at least 2 cm specimens sectioned at 1 mm intervals.

The following caveats should be kept in mind when treating these patients:

- The headache responds to treatment *within 48 hours* in most cases. Failure to respond within 5 to 7 days should prompt re-evaluation of the diagnosis.
- All patients require treatment. Blindness does not occur only with *severe* arteritis.
- Treatment with low-dose maintenance steroids after a very gradual taper is often required. Recurrences have been reported.
- Steroid dose requirement will depend on maintained normalization of the ESR and/or acute phase reactants, as well as a review of the patient's ocular, masticatory, systemic, and headache symptoms.

Other systemic arteritides such as systemic lupus erythematosus, polyarteritis nodosa, and Wegener's granulomatosis may also present with headache as a major feature. Focal neurologic deficits, seizures, behavioral and cognitive dysfunction, and arterial stroke occur in conjunction with other evidence of *systemic markers of inflammation* and *visceral organ involvement.*

One noteworthy exception is isolated CNS (granulomatous) vasculitis. This uncommon disorder is a noninfectious recurrent angiopathy confined to the CNS; it is usually fatal if left untreated. The most common presenting symptom is headache, which is usually severe and either acute or progressive. Mental symptoms and seizures are common, and focal or multifocal neurologic deficits develop in over 90% of cases. Importantly, constitutional symptoms are usually absent, and there are no systemic markers of inflammation or visceral organ involvement. The outcome can be favorable when treated with prednisone and cyclophosphamide.

MENINGEAL HEADACHES

Headache is often the presenting, most prominent, and sometimes the only symptom of conditions that primarily involve the leptomeninges (arachnoid and dura mater). Meningoencephalitides may be caused by:

- Infections (bacterial and viral, including HIV)
- Neoplasm (carcinomatous meningitis, lymphoma)
- Granulomatous disease (sarcoid, TB)

- Blood (subarachnoid hemorrhage)
- Chemical or irritative substances (drugs such as carbamazepine and NSAIDs)
- Intracranial lesions which leak irritative substances into the subarachnoid space (epidermoid cysts and craniopharyngioma) may also cause meningeal inflammation and headache.

Headache is the commonest symptom of infectious meningitis. It is often the first symptom to occur and may be the last symptom to remain as a long-term complication. A rapid onset headache with progressive severity accompanied by fever, meningismus, photophobia, and altered level of consciousness requires little diagnostic prowess. The diagnosis may be more difficult and clinical presentations more variable depending on the microorganism involved, the age of the patient, and the immunocompetency of the host. In the very young or old and in immunocompromised patients, a subacute or chronic presentation betrays the characteristic fulminant onset the clinician anticipates.

In the absence of focal neurologic signs, a prompt CSF examination is essential when the following features are present:

- Acute or subacute headache with fever (even low grade)
- Meningismus (despite how subtle)
- Photophobia, irritability, myalgias, anorexia, vomiting
- Signs of systemic infection (cough, corrhyza, dysuria, leukocytosis, elevated ESR)
- Lethargy, altered awareness or behavior

Tables 11.1 and 11.2 outline the appropriate CSF tests and treatment depending on the host and organism.

Table 11.1   The CSF in Meningeal Headache

CSF Examination

- opening pressure
- cell count and differential*
- glucose (with concomitant serum glucose)†
- protein
- gram stain and culture (don't forget blood cultures as well)

Rapid Diagnostic Tests

- latex agglutination (encapsulated organisms)
- limulus amebocyte lysate (gram-negative organisms)
- lactate (>3.5mmol/L - bacterial meningitis)

*Note that in the very young, very old, or immunocompromised host, a pleocytosis may be absent.
†CSF glucose <50% of blood glucose is suggestive of purulent bacterial meningitis.

Table 11.2 Antibiotics for Bacterial Meningitis

Recommended Antimicrobial Agent Based on Age and Organism	
Neonates	**Antimicrobial**
Group B streptococci	Penicillin G or ampicillin
E. coli	Cefotaxime or ceftriaxone
Children	
H. influenza type b	Cefotaxime or ceftriaxone
N. meningitidis	Penicillin G or ampicillin
Adults	
S. pneumonia	Penicillin G or ampicillin or ceftriaxone
N. meningitidis	Penicillin G or ampicillin or ceftriaxone
Gram-negative bacilli	3rd generation cephalosporin
P. aeruginosa	Ceftazidime
H. influenza	3rd generation cephalosporin
S. aureus (methicillin sensitive)	Nafcillin or oxacillin
S. aureus (methicillin resistant)	Vancomycin
Staphylococci (coagulase negative)	Vancomycin
Listeria monocytogenes	Ampicillin (plus aminoglyside)

Dexamethasone is recommended in the pediatric population to minimize or avert neurologic morbidity. Recommendations for adults cannot be definitively made, but preliminary results appear favorable. The medication should be given 15 to 20 minutes prior to antibiotic therapy, at a dose of 0.15 mg/kg every 6 hours intravenously for 4 days.

OROMANDIBULAR DYSFUNCTION

Headache as a major symptom of oromandibular dysfunction (OMD) is felt to be relatively uncommon. When headache or facial pain is secondary to dental (pulpal or periodontal) pathology, local intraoral symptomatology rarely poses a diagnostic dilemma.

Headache as a symptom of temporomandibular disorders (TMD) is more controversial. Symptoms or signs of TMD may occur in up to 70% of the population. Despite this, it is estimated that less than 5% require treatment and even fewer have headache. The most common etiologic factors for headache associated with TMD include myofascial pain, bruxism, trauma, occlusal interferences, and emotional stressors.

The pain associated with TMD is most commonly myofascial, but may in some cases be related to internal derangement or inflammation of the joint. TMD as an etiologic factor for headache should only be considered if the following characteristics are present:

- Mild to moderate pain localized to or radiating from the joint
- Jaw pain is precipitated by movement and/or clenching with associated tenderness of the joint capsule

- Crepitus and/or decreased range of motion with jaw opening/closure
- X-rays or tomographic images of the joint may show derangement of the joint.

The clinician confronted with facial pain must be aware of the following headache disorders which often cause pain in the region of oromandibular structures:

- Migraine
- Cluster headache
- Chronic paroxysmal hemicrania
- Trigeminal neuralgia.

SINUS-RELATED HEADACHES

Headache as a manifestation of sinus pathology is an overemphasized entity and is often erroneously implicated in patients suffering from migraine, tension-type, and cluster headaches. Sinus disorders such as allergic and vasomotor rhinitis, nasal polyposis, and congenital or acquired anatomic variations are common in the general population, but extraordinarily uncommon as a direct cause for chronic headache.

Headache and facial pain usually occurs early and simultaneously with the acute stage of *purulent* sinusitis. Headache location varies depending on the individual sinus affected. There is usually a purulent nasal discharge, tenderness over the sinus (especially with maxillary and frontal sinusitis), and pathologic findings on either x-ray or CT imaging, or transillumination.

Rhinogenic headache is as uncommon as sinus pathology as a cause for chronic headache, but in appropriate circumstances, the following should be excluded:

- Septal impaction or contact with the lateral nasal wall from a nasal "spur" with or without nasal obstruction
- Post-traumatic septal hematomas
- Nasal/nasopharyngeal tumors.

The associated headache is usually frontal or facial in location, mild to moderate in severity, dull, deep, nonpulsatile, and associated with a heaviness or fullness.

Headache as a major feature of allergic or vasomotor rhinitis, turbinate hypertrophy, atrophic sinus membranes, and chronic sinusitis is not validated and care should be taken before invasive diagnostic or therapeutic intervention is undertaken.

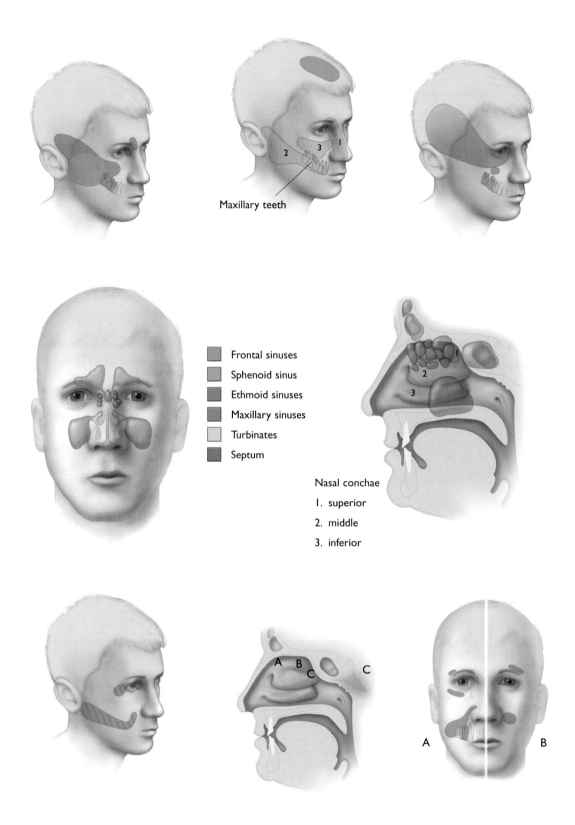

Maxillary teeth

Frontal sinuses
Sphenoid sinus
Ethmoid sinuses
Maxillary sinuses
Turbinates
Septum

Nasal conchae

1. superior
2. middle
3. inferior

Figure 11.1   The letters A, B, C, indicate areas where pain is felt when the corresponding numbered areas of the superior nasal cavity are stimulated.

Sphenoid sinusitis represents a notable exception to the rule that sinusitis is a rare cause of chronic headache. The clinician should be alert to this diagnosis in patients who present with a subacute and progressive frontal or retro-orbital headache which may be associated with chemosis, proptosis, and oculomotor palsies, even in the absence of fever or leukocytosis. This entity may be overlooked clinically and radiographically unless a specific "sinus CT" is requested.

Bibliography

Bengtsson BA, Malmvall BE. Giant cell arteritis. Acta Medica Scand 1982; (Suppl 658):1–102.

Girgis NI, Farid Z, Mikhail IA, et al. Dexamethasone treatment for bacterial meningitis in children and adults. Pediatr Infect Dis J 1989; 8:848–851.

Solberg WK, Graff-Radford SB. Orodental considerations in facial pain. Semin Neurol 1988; 8:318.

Supplementary Search Strategies

SuSS 1

Subject	explode Headache (index term) or headache (text word)
Subject	Temporal Arteritis or explode Vasculitis (index term) or vasculitis (text word) (index term)
Limited to	1994 through 1997

SuSS 2

Subject	explode Headache (index term) or headache (text word)
Subject	explode Meningitis (index term) or meningitis (text word)
Limited to	1994 through 1997

SuSS 3

Subject	explode Headache (index term) or headache (text word)
Subject	explode Temporomandibular Joint (index term) or explode Temporomandibular Joint Disorders (index term)
Limited to	1994 through 1997

SuSS 4

Subject	explode Headache (index term) or headache (text word)
Subject	explode Paranasal Sinus Diseases (index term) or Paranasal Sinuses (index term) or sinus:(text word)
Limited to	1994 through 1997

Chapter 12

CRANIAL NEURALGIAS AND FACIAL PAIN

Neuralgia refers to pain felt in the distribution of a particular nerve, or nerve root. Signature characteristics of the pain include its intermittency, brevity, severity, explosive onset, and electric shock-like or lancinating qualities. The function of the involved nerve is normal, with postherpetic neuralgia as the notable exception. The vast majority of cranial neuralgias are idiopathic.

TRIGEMINAL NEURALGIA

Trigeminal neuralgia is the prototypical cranial neuralgia. It is a painful unilateral affliction of the face characterized by brief, electric shock-like pains limited to the distribution of one or more divisions of the trigeminal nerve, almost always V_2 and/or V_3. Pain that wanders or spreads to involve the ear, occiput, neck or chest, should cast doubt on the diagnosis. The pain intensity is invariably severe, and often characterized as sudden, sharp, superficial, stabbing, or burning in quality. The pain may occur spontaneously, but more often is evoked by trivial facial stimuli including washing, shaving, talking, brushing the teeth, eating, or a gentle breeze on the face. The painful volleys of paroxysms often last less than 20 to 30 seconds (often 3 to 5 seconds) and are separated by pain-free periods lasting seconds to hours. The evoked pain often occurs in association with trigger zones especially about the nostrils and mouth.

Although a dull aching discomfort lasting hours may follow a particularly intense or prolonged series of painful paroxysms, suspicion about a secondary cause should arise when the paroxysms of pain punctuate a more continuous dull aching pain, and when symptoms or signs of trigeminal nerve dysfunction are present.

Compression, distortion, disruption, or stretching of trigeminal nerve root fibers by a branch of either the anterior or posterior inferior cerebellar artery is the usual cause of idiopathic trigeminal neuralgia. It is very important to bear in mind that even when the description of the pain is classical, an underlying structural intracranial abnormality may be lurking. Recent studies with large numbers of patients suggest that 10% of patients harbour a brain tumor. This underscores the necessity to obtain an MRI on *every* patient with trigeminal neuralgia, even in those who respond to medication and whose examination is normal.

Medical Therapy

When initiating therapy for trigeminal neuralgia, it is wise to remember that spontaneous remissions are the rule, with 50% of patients achieving a remission of 6 months or more. Medical therapy need not therefore be indefinite. After 6 to 8 weeks of freedom from pain, a drug taper over a similar time period is reasonable.

The treatment of first choice is carbamazepine, 100 to 200 mg b.i.d. The dose is escalated by 200 mg increments every 2 to 3 days until efficacy or until dose-limiting side effects occur. A response usually occurs within 48 hours and a typical maintenance dose is 600 to 1200 mg. Dizziness, anorexia, sedation, or ataxia in isolation or combination may develop. Less than 10% of patients will be intolerant. The least common but most feared adverse event is aplastic anemia. Reversible leukopenia or thrombocytopenia may occur in about 2% of patients. Baseline LFTs should be done prior to starting this medication and monitored according to the prescribing guidelines.

If the response to carbamazepine is inadequate, lioresal can be an especially useful adjunctive agent. It can be used successfully as monotherapy and may in some cases be the preferred agent. The usual starting dose is 5 to 10 mg t.i.d. The typical maintenance dosage is 60 to 80 mg per day in divided doses.

Phenytoin has traditionally been the second-line agent but the response rate is estimated to be only 25%. An oral loading dose of 1 g in divided doses over a 24-hour period followed by 300 to 400 mg per day is a typical starting regimen. Phenytoin may be particularly useful in the acute setting when the pain is proving refractory to treatment, or while the patient is awaiting surgery. In this setting, phenytoin can be given intravenously at a dose of 250 to 500 mg over 20 to 30 minutes. There are numerous medications which can be helpful in selected cases. These include clonazepam, pimozide, valproate, gabapentin, lamotrigine, and misoprostol.

Once the patient has proven refractory to the first three agents employed at adequate doses and in rational combinations, surgical therapy is usually the next best treatment option. Unfortunately, despite best medical efforts, 25 to 50% of patients will fail to repond to all pharmacological attempts, and pain relief ultimately requires a surgical procedure.

Treatment of Cranial Neuralgia

Carbamazepine
Initial: 100 mg b.i.d.
Maintenance: 600 mg–1200 mg/day
Warning: aplastic anemia, leukopenia,
thrombocytopenia, hepatic
dysfunction

No | Effective | Yes

Continue until pain-
free for eight weeks;
then gradual taper
(8 weeks)

Lioresal (baclofen)
Initial: 5–10 mg b.i.d.
Maintenance:
30–80 mg/day

or

Phenytoin
Initial: oral load over 24 hours
(1 g) Maintenance: 300–600 mg/day
Warning: hypersensitivity
reactions

A

If neither effective,
combination therapy
(Lioresal + Carbamazine)

Refractory to
medical therapy

Effective

Effective

Continue until pain-
free for eight weeks,
then taper each
medication slowly
in succession

B

Continue until
pain-free for eight
weeks, then gradual
(8 weeks) taper

C

Surgical referral:
• Glycerol gangliolysis
• Radiofrequency gangliolysis
• Microvascular decompression
• Radiosurgery ("Gamma knife")

Critical Decisions

A

If combination therapy is not tolerated, effective, or advisable, other pharmacological options include:
• clonazepam (3–8 mg/day)
• pimozide (4–12 mg/day)
• valproate (500–2000 mg/day)
• gabapentin (900–1800 mg/day)

B

Recall: 50% of patients experience remission >6 mo and 25% > 1yr.

C

The most appropriate surgical procedure will depend on patient's age, medical comorbidities, etc.

Surgery

Since 30% of patients will fail medical therapy, surgical treatment can be thought of as part of a stepwise approach to management. Radiofrequency trigeminal rhizotomy, glycerol gangliolysis, and microvascular decompression have become safe and effective alternatives to render these patients pain-free. Radiofrequency lesions and glycerol injections enjoy similar long-term success rates (60 to 85%) with acceptable operative morbidity. Facial sensory loss may occur with both procedures. Fortunately, corneal anasthesia, anasthesia dolorosa, dysesthesias and masseter weakness, are uncommon adverse events. Although there are pros and cons unique to each procedure, glycerol injections are less selective for the individual trigeminal branches and analgesia may not be as complete.

Microvascular decompression is felt to be the definitive procedure for trigeminal neuralgia, but it is usually reserved for intractable cases and the rare instances of V_1 distribution pain. The procedure involves a posterior craniectomy and segregation of the trigeminal root from a juxtaposed or adherent blood vessel, resulting in pain relief in over 90% of patients.

Radiosurgery

The "Gamma Knife" is a device used to perform "stereotactic radiosurgery," a technique that projects 201 very fine beams of gamma rays, generated by radioactive cobalt, through the skull to perform the equivalent of a surgical procedure without opening the skull. Recent evidence suggests that Gamma Knife focused on the root of the trigeminal nerve, is comparable both in efficiency and side-effect profile, with these other more invasive surgical approaches to this disorder.

OTHER CRANIAL NEURALGIAS

There are a few rare neuralgias of unknown etiology ("idiopathic"), including glossopharyngeal, geniculate, and superior laryngeal neuralgias (Figure 12.1). Because the sensory innervation to the ear, pharynx, tonsil, tongue, and jaw may overlap (CN V, VII, IX, X) and converge within the brain stem (nucleus tractus solitarius and spinal nucleus of V), these neuralgias may be difficult to distinguish from each other. The pain characteristics and treatment are the same as for trigeminal neuralgia, but the prevalence is much lower and the locations distinctively different. Although idiopathic in most instances like trigeminal neuralgia, structural causes always require exclusion.

Three characteristic neuralgic syndromes require special consideration since the therapeutic approach is considerably different from trigeminal neuralgia.

The first is *occipital neuralgia,* which presents as a stabbing pain, often accompanied by diminished sensation and dysesthesias felt in the distribution of the greater or lesser occipital nerves. Often there is local tenderness over the nerve at the skull base, which on palpation may reproduce a typical paroxysm of pain. Local infiltration of an anesthetic (0.5% bupivicaine) at this point of tenderness will usually relieve the pain and can be diagnostic. If so, a concomitant local corticosteroid (Depo-medrol®) injection may provide temporary, and in some cases, longstanding relief.

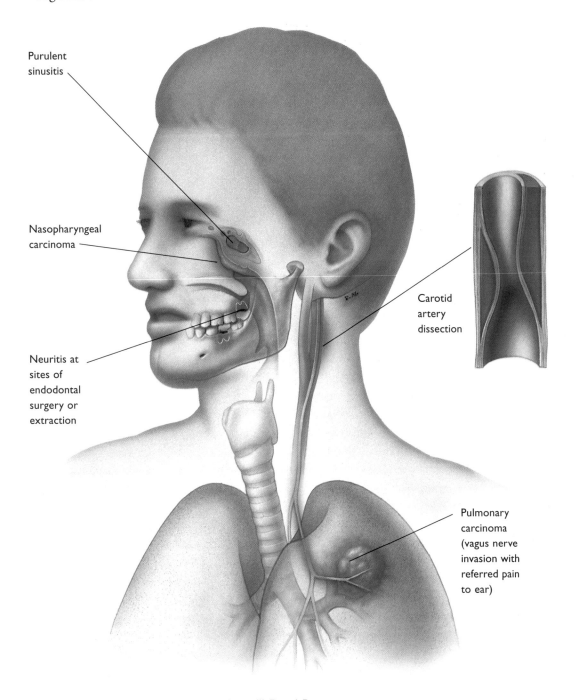

Purulent
sinusitis

Nasopharyngeal
carcinoma

Neuritis at
sites of
endodontal
surgery or
extraction

Carotid
artery
dissection

Pulmonary
carcinoma
(vagus nerve
invasion with
referred pain
to ear)

Figure 12.1 Sources of "Unexplained" Facial Pain

Postherpetic neuralgia may occur in the distribution of a division of the trigeminal nerve (25% of cases involve CN V) which has been affected by herpes zoster. Nearly always it is the first division of the trigeminal nerve that is involved. The pain by definition persists for more than 6 months after the herpetic eruption has resolved. The pain is constant and boring with superimposed flashes of knife-like pain, and with paroxysms of sharp pain induced by normally innocuous stimulation (allodynia). Early treatment with acyclovir (800 mg five times per day for 7 days) and prednisone (3 week tapering schedule starting at 60 mg) has been shown to accelerate healing and reduce the duration of pain. Symptomatic treatment for chronic cases usually includes tricyclic antidepressants (amitriptyline or nortriptyline), beginning at low doses, since the individuals at risk are elderly and the side effects potentially more prominent. A starting dose of 10 to 25 mg with a maintenance dose of 50 to 75 mg is usual. Topical agents may be effective alone or when combined with a tricyclic. Capsaicin (0.075%) applied to the affected area four times per day for 4 weeks or ASA (325 mg) emulsified in chloroform (20 cc) and applied three times per day has proven efficacy and can be very useful as adjunctive treatments.

SUNCT (Short-lasting, Unilateral, Neuralgiform headache attacks with Conjunctival injection, Tearing, rhinorrhea, and forehead sweating) is a unilateral syndrome characterized by neuralgiform pain of short duration (15 to 120 seconds). These ocular or periocular paroxysms of pain can be triggered by cutaneous stimuli or neck movement and occur with a frequency ranging from 1 or 2 per day to 10 to 30 per hour. There is a male preponderance. Patients are typically pain-free between paroxysms. Unlike trigeminal neuralgia, the pain is exclusively in the distribution of the first trigeminal division and carbamazepine is rarely effective. The brevity and frequency of individual attacks and lack of response to corticosteroids, calcium channel blockers, and sumatriptan, distinguish this syndrome from cluster. Overall, no drug has shown lasting efficacy in this syndrome although anecdotal reports of pain relief with corticosteroids, sumatriptan, and carbamazepine are available.

ATYPICAL FACIAL PAIN

This term should be avoided. It not only has become equated with psychopathology, but sinister underlying causes may be overlooked if this "diagnosis" is relied upon (see Fig. 12.1).

As the name implies, the pain characteristics differ from the major cranial neuralgias discussed previously in the following ways:

- Steady, boring, burning, throbbing diffuse pain—not neuralgic
- Pain persists for hours, days, or months—not brief paroxysms with pain-free intervals
- No trigger zones
- No precipitants (washing, brushing teeth, chewing, swallowing, etc.)
- More commonly seen in a younger age group and more frequent in women
- Pain is not relieved with anticonvulsants or ablative procedures of the fifth or ninth cranial nerve
- Areas of localized tenderness with spread of pain to other areas of the face, cranium, or neck.

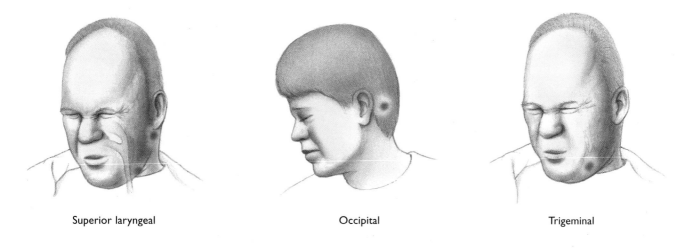

Superior laryngeal   Occipital   Trigeminal

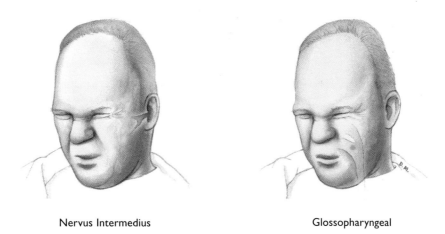

Nervus Intermedius   Glossopharyngeal

Figure 12.2   **Areas of Facial Neuralgia. Red:superficial area of pain; Blue: deep (internal) area of pain.**

Critical Decisions

A Brain MRI
- Brain MRI with contrast should be performed on all patients presenting with new onset facial pain.
- Also applies to patients with "classic" trigeminal neuralgia, since underlying mass lesion may mimic even the most classic of headache or facial pain syndromes.

B Migraine and cluster headaches
- May present as facial pain, or in the case of cluster, may present as intraoral pain also.
- Chronic paroxysmal hemicrania (CPH) and episodic paroxysmal hemicrania (EPH) are peculiar headache syndromes characterized by short attacks of severe unilateral orbital pain lasting approximately 20 minutes (2–45 min.), with a frequency of about five per day (140/day). They are associated with ipsilateral autonomic features such as lacrimation, conjunctival injection, rhinorrhea, nasal congestion or ptosis.
- CPH and EPH have an abrupt, sustained, and often absolute response to indomethacin.

C Other cranial neuralgia
- Neuralgic pain occurring in an "extra-trigeminal" location is often diagnosed on the basis of the location of the pain (see Fig. 12.2).

D SUNCT syndrome
- SUNCT syndrome refers to a recently described headache syndrome featuring brief paroxysms of severe lancinating periorbital or retroorbital pain (10–60 seconds), that have a frequency ranging from less than one per day to 30 per hour, and the attacks are accompanied by prominent ipsilateral conjunctival injection, tearing, rhinorrhea, and nasal obstruction.
- SUNCT syndrome has a male predominance (4:1).

E ENT and dental assessment
- Should be done before diagnosis of atypical or idiopathic facial pain is rendered to exclude disorders such as nasopharyngeal carcinoma, sinusitis, rhinologic causes for facial pain, temporal mandibular dysfunction and intra-oral pathology.

Evaluation of Facial Pain

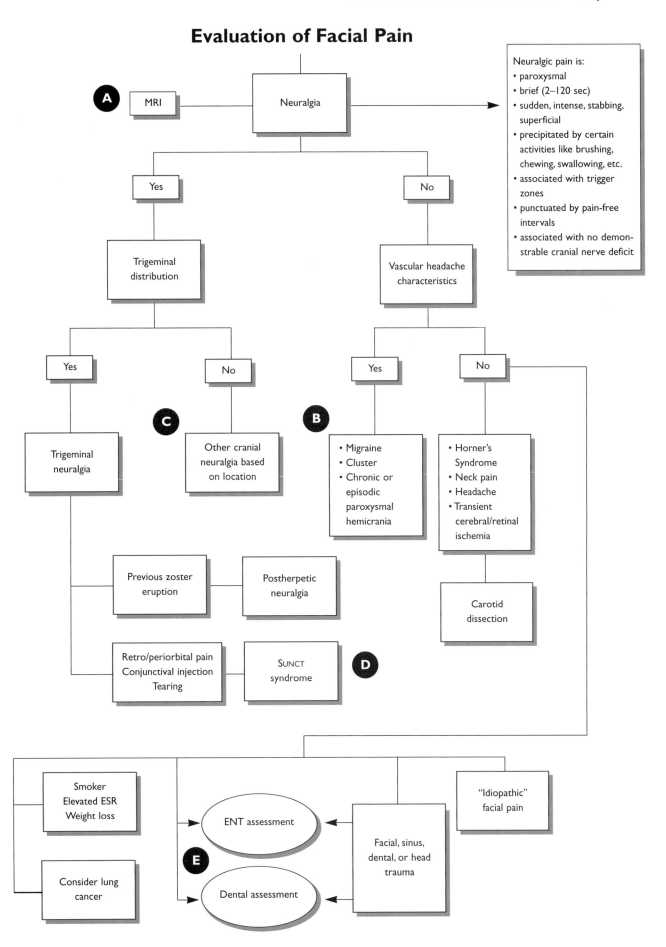

A — MRI → Neuralgia →

Neuralgic pain is:
- paroxysmal
- brief (2–120 sec)
- sudden, intense, stabbing, superficial
- precipitated by certain activities like brushing, chewing, swallowing, etc.
- associated with trigger zones
- punctuated by pain-free intervals
- associated with no demonstrable cranial nerve deficit

Yes

Trigeminal distribution

Yes — No

Trigeminal neuralgia

C

Other cranial neuralgia based on location

Previous zoster eruption — Postherpetic neuralgia

Retro/periorbital pain
Conjunctival injection
Tearing — SUNCT syndrome   **D**

No

Vascular headache characteristics

Yes — No

B

- Migraine
- Cluster
- Chronic or episodic paroxysmal hemicrania

- Horner's Syndrome
- Neck pain
- Headache
- Transient cerebral/retinal ischemia

Carotid dissection

Smoker
Elevated ESR
Weight loss

Consider lung cancer

ENT assessment

E

Dental assessment

Facial, sinus, dental, or head trauma

"Idiopathic" facial pain

A diligent search for disease of the sinuses, teeth, pharynx, temporomandibular joint, and chest is required in all patients. In addition, characteristics which might suggest a vascular headache cause should be sought. A diagnosis of "atypical facial pain" can only be made after exclusion of the following possibilities:

- Nasopharyngeal carcinoma
- Pulmonary carcinoma (invasion of the ipsilateral vagus nerve)
- Mandibular or maxillary bone abscesses (at site of previous tooth extractions)
- Mandibular or maxillary neuritis (at site of endodontal root canal surgery, or extractions)
- Sinusitis (including ethmoidal and sphenoidal sinusitis)
- Carotidynia and carotid artery dissection
- Post-traumatic facial pain, which sometimes follows surgical procedures such as sinus procedures, dental extractions, and orbital enucleations
- Vascular features that suggest migraine ("lower half migraine"), or autonomic and cyclical features characteristic of cluster ("Ekbom's lower half headache").

Diagnostic evaluation of non-neuralgic facial pain should include:

1. Baseline hematologic assessment (CBC, ESR) and chemistry panel
2. ENT evaluation (MRI head to exclude nasopharyngeal carcinoma, or coronal sinus CT may be indicated.)
3. Dental evaluation (TMJ dysfunction, mandibular or maxillary bone cavities)
4. Chest film (CT chest if index of suspicion is high—weight loss, smoking history, increased ESR).

Treatment of non-neuralgic facial pain is directed at the primary cause.

If no obvious source is uncovered, the tricyclics are the mainstay of treatment. Various agents such as lioresal, clonidine, MAO inhibitors, narcotics, and nonpharmacologic modalities such as biobehavioral techniques and sympathetic blockade have been tried, but their use and rational combination requires referral to an experienced center or pain specialist.

Bibliography

Bernstein JE, Korman NJ, Bickers DR, et al. Topical capsaicin in postherpetic neuralgia. J Am Acad Dermatol 1989; 21:265–270.

Capobianco DJ. Facial pain as a symptom of nonmetastatic lung cancer. Headache 1995; 35:581–585.

Fields HL. Treatment of trigeminal neuralgia. NEIM. 1996:334(17); 1125–1126

Fromm GH. Pathophysiology of trigeminal neuralgia. In: Fromm GH, Sessle BJ, eds. Trigeminal neuralgia current concepts regarding pathogenesis and treatment. Boston: Butterworth-Heinemann, 1991:105–122.

Hakanson S. Surgical treatment: retrogasserian ganglion glycerol injection. In: Fromm GH, Sessle BJ, eds. Trigeminal neuralgia current concepts regarding pathogenesis and treatment. Boston: Butterworth-Heinemann, 1991:185–204.

Jannetta PJ. Surgical treatment: microvascular decompression. In: Fromm GH, Sessle BJ, eds. Trigeminal neuralgia current concepts regarding pathogenesis and treatment. Boston: Butterworth-Heinemann, 1991:145–157.

King RB. Topical aspirin in chloroform and the relief of pain due to herpes zoster and postherpetic neuralgia. Arch Neurol 1993; 50:1046–1053.

Kreczkes K, Basheer AM. Do corticosteroids prevent post-herpetic neuralgia? Br J Dermatol 1980; 102:551–555.

McKendrick MW, McGill JI, White JE, et al. Oral acyclovir in acute herpes zoster. BMJ 1986; 293:1529–1532.

Pareja JA, Kruszewski P, Sjaastad O. SUNCT syndrome: trials of drugs and anesthetic blockades. Headache 1995; 35:138–142.

Terrence CF, Fromm GH. Trigeminal neuralgia and other facial neuralgias. In: Oleson J, Tfelt-Hanson P, Welch KMA, eds. The headaches. New York: Raven Press, 1993.

Young RF, Vermeulen SS, Grimm P, Blasko J, Posewitz A. Gamma knife radiosurgery for treatment of trigeminal neuralgia. Neurology 1997; 48:608–614.

Supplementary Search Strategy

SuSS I	
Subject	explode Headache (index term) or headache (text word)
Subject	Facial Pain (index term) or Trigeminal Neuralgia (index term)
Limited to	1994 through 1997

Chapter 13

HEADACHES OF
CEREBROVASCULAR ORIGIN

Of all the cranial structures, the blood vessels are among the most sensitive to pain (Figure 13.1). Neurogenic dysfunction of the cranial vasculature is believed to be responsible for the production of that very common headache, migraine. Not surprisingly, lesions or diseases of these blood vessels may also commonly cause headache. "Commonly" requires definition. Some diseases, though themselves rare, nearly always are associated with prominent headache; examples are intracranial venous occlusion, and vasculitis. Other diseases, though quite common, produce headaches in only about one-quarter of cases, and these often are a minor concern to the patient in comparison with the accompanying neurologic deficit (such as paralysis); an example is atherosclerotic cerebral ischemia. Still other conditions, such as subarachnoid hemorrhage, are neither common nor rare, but nearly always cause severe headache when they occur. The following enumerates those cerebrovascular conditions presenting with headache, in the approximate order of their frequency in a general practice.

- Subarachnoid hemorrhage: aneurysmal leaks and ruptures, arteriovenous malformations (AVM), other rare causes.
- Parenchymal brain hemorrhage: cerebral and cerebellar hemorrhages from hypertension and other rare causes: e.g., aneurysm, AVM, bleeding diatheses.
- Severe hypertension: hypertensive crises from uncontrolled essential hypertension, drug reactions or, rarely, pheochromocytoma; early morning headaches from uncontrolled hypertension.
- Cranial vasculitis: giant cell (temporal) arteritis, other vasculitides.
- Intracranial veno-occlusive disease.
- Arterial dissection.
- Atherosclerotic and embolic cerebrovascular ischemic disease.

Recognizing these headaches for what they are—warnings of ominous disease—is a major concern for the primary care physician.

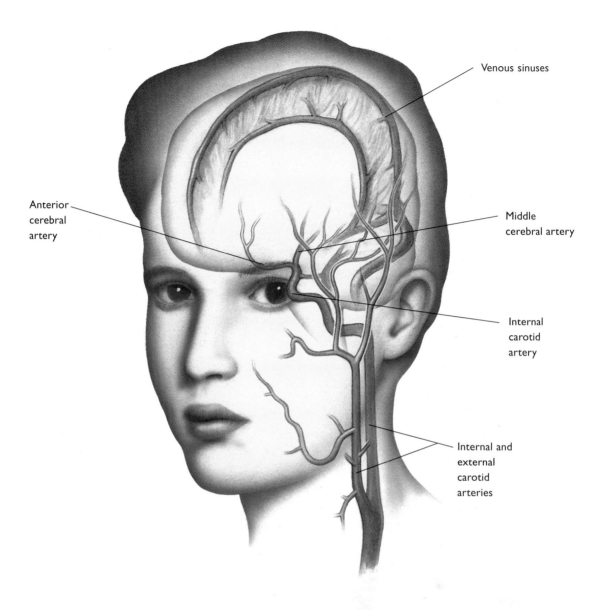

Venous sinuses

Anterior cerebral artery

Middle cerebral artery

Internal carotid artery

Internal and external carotid arteries

Figure 13.1 Vascular Pain-Sensitive Structures

Subarachnoid Hemorrhage

Subarachnoid hemorrhage is easy to recognize in its full-blown form. The cataclysmic onset of devastating headache, the collapse, the board-like stiffness of the neck, and the unmistakeable appearance of grave illness, all proclaim the diagnosis. Sometimes, however, the subarachnoid hemorrhage is not massive. A small amount of blood leaking from an aneurysm or an AVM into the subarachnoid space can produce a sudden and severe but not overwhelming headache; the patient may be able to stay on his or her feet and keep moving about; nuchal rigidity may be equivocal or even absent; and, though evidently sick, the patient may not seem seriously ill. The appearance may be similar to a severe attack of the patient's habitual migraine. The "subarachnoid leak," or "sentinel hemorrhage," or "warning bleed," however we name it, is the stuff of medical nightmares.

How do you recognize it? The key is to consider subarachnoid hemorrhage in any patient with the sudden (absent one moment, present the next) onset of severe headache. In such cases, check for the following:

Onset during Exertion. Though aneurysms and AVMs can leak at any time, they are more likely to do so during lifting, straining, intercourse, or exercise. (Benign headaches may also be triggered by these activities, but should never be dismissed as such until subarachnoid hemorrhage has been excluded.)

Nuchal Rigidity ("Stiff Neck"). This can be absent, but more often than not is present if tested for properly.

Subhyaloid Hemorrhages in the Optic Fundi. Though not a common finding, these are incontrovertible evidence of subarachnoid hemorrhage. No examination of a headache patient is complete without fundoscopy.

Other Neurologic Abnormalities. These include alteration of consciousness or behavior (however slight), pupillary abnormalities (an aneurysm at the junction of the internal carotid and posterior communicating arteries may present with a painful partial third nerve palsy affecting especially the pupil), or any other abnormal sign.

In general, young people (most aneurysms rupture after the age of 35) whose acute severe headaches are settling down without analgesics, who did not have their headaches come on with exertion, who are and have been perfectly alert and oriented, and who on repeated examinations have no neurologic abnormalities or neck stiffness, are at low risk of having had a subarachnoid hemorrhage. All others with acute severe headaches need to have subarachnoid hemorrhage excluded by an unenhanced computed tomography (CT) scan of the head, followed by lumbar puncture if the CT scan fails to show any hemorrhage. The primary care physician can best do this by referring the patient immediately to the Emergency Department for urgent consultation.

Parenchymal Brain Hemorrhage

Parenchymal brain hemorrhage is much easier to diagnose because the hemorrhage, as it plows through the substance of the brain, creates obvious neurologic problems such as hemiplegia, speech disturbances, and vertigo. These patients are often older than patients with benign dysfunctional headaches, and they may be hypertensive, because high blood pressure is the most common cause of intracerebral hemorrhage. Look for the patient with sudden onset headache with a neurologic deficit. Remember, though, that a small intracerebral hemorrhage may not cause headache, and may be mistaken for a "thrombotic stroke."

High Blood Pressure

Contrary to medical mythology, high blood pressure only rarely causes headache. Most people with high blood pressure and headaches have the same tension-type and migraine headaches as their normotensive neighbors. Only very high blood pressure (diastolic > 120) causes headache, and it may do so in three ways:

1. Chronic severe hypertension can produce a dull throbbing occipital headache that is present when the patient awakens in the morning, and then slowly fades as the patient gets up and about. These "early morning headaches" resemble the headaches of increased intracranial pressure; it may be that disturbed vasomotor autoregulation in the head leads to intracranial vascular congestion which may be augmented by the supine position and any nocturnal carbon dioxide retention.

2. Acute hypertensive crises may present as sudden generalized severe headache, likely due to acute collapse of intracranial autoregulation. (Remember to exclude the possibility of subarachnoid hemorrage in these cases.) While textbooks give pheochromocytomas as the typical cause, in these days much likelier causes are cocaine, amphetamines, and the inadvertent consumption of pressor agents such as decongestants by people taking monoamine oxidase inhibitors.

3. Acute hypertensive encephalopathy is a rare complication of chronic severe hypertension, and presents as headache, obtundation, seizures, papilledema, and/or multifocal neurologic deficits. There is a scattered segmental failure of protective vasoconstriction by the cerebral vasculature, with multifocal areas of cerebral congestion, edema, infarction, and hemorrhage.

Remember, if the diastolic blood pressure is elevated, but is less than 120, by all means treat the hypertension—but look for another cause of the patient's headaches.

Cranial Vasculitis

Cranial vasculitis typically presents as headache, often in the initial absence of any neurologic abnormalities. The commonest type of cranial vasculitis is giant cell or temporal arteritis, and most primary care physicians can expect to see a few cases in their careers. These patients, unlike most patients with benign dysfunctional headaches, experience the onset of their headaches after the age of 50 years. Again, unlike most patients with benign dysfunctional headaches, these people are not otherwise well. Careful enquiry will elicit symptoms suggestive of the generalized collagen-vascular disease that they harbor: malaise, febrility, aching back and leg muscles (polymyalgia rheumatica), joint pains, weight loss, jaw claudication (aching of the jaw muscles as they chew), and, ominously, episodic visual failure caused by arteritis of the vessels supplying the optic nerve and retina. Examination may reveal a general appearance of illness, perhaps a low-grade fever, and some-times local changes in the scalp arteries (classically, the temporal arteries) consist-ing of tenderness, swelling, and impaired pulsatility. Laboratory studies usually support the clinical suspicion of a generalized process. Typically (at least 85% of the time) the erythrocyte sedimentation rate (ESR) is unequivocally elevated. Less often there is a mild leukocytosis, a slight normocytic anemia, or other nonspecific systemic reverberations of inflammation. Untreated, the prognosis is bleak; within a year of developing headache, 50% of patients with giant cell arteritis, untreated, will go on to develop a major vascular complication of their disease, often blind-ness. Corticosteroids markedly improve the outcome; given in a dose sufficient to keep the patient asymptomatic and the ESR normal, they control the disease. Corticosteroids, generally speaking, are a long-term treatment, not devoid of com-plications, and thus usually should not be given unless temporal artery biopsy con-firms the diagnosis. Again, if the primary care physician suspects this diagnosis, the prudent play is a very quick punt to the specialist.

Other vasculitides, such as polyarteritis nodosa, lupus, and so on, may also cause headaches. As with giant cell arteritis, they are almost always associated with systemic signs and symptoms of the primary disease. There is a very rare disease, primary intracranial angiitis, which is unassociated with any evidence of systemic arteritis, and may not be associated until later with neurologic symptoms or signs. It is extremely difficult to diagnose. Look for a patient of any age (but usually mid-dle-aged) with a new onset persistent headache, which does not conform to the profile of migraine or tension-type headache; and refer this patient to a specialist for investigation. Often, the specialist has difficulty clinching the diagnosis, even with resort to MRI to show the brain parenchymal effects of vasculitis, CSF examination to uncover the cytologic and chemical reverberations of intracranial inflammation, and cerebral angiography to display morphologic changes in the blood vessels. A brain biopsy is the gold standard for securing a definitive diagnosis. Sometimes, especially when the patient is incurring cumulative neurologic deficits, the neurologist has to start corticosteroid or other immunosuppressant treatment without the reassurance of a proven diagnosis.

Intracranial Veno-Occlusive Disease

Though itself rare, intracranial veno-occlusive disease almost always causes headache when it occurs. Early reports of this entity stressed as causes mastoid and sinus infections, trauma, dehydration, sepsis, pregnancy, and the postpartum state. These are still the most common causes in the third world, but in Europe and North America intracranial venous sinus thrombosis more frequently results from coagulopathies (such as antiphospholipid antibody syndrome, polycythemia, homocystinuria, paraneoplastic state, activated protein C resistance), secondary hyperosmolarity, dehydration, and (still in a few cases) the puerperium. These causes, except of course for the puerperium, may not be obvious when the patient presents with neurologic problems.

Headache is usually prominent. The headache may be insidious and progressive, or may mimic the "thunderclap" onset of a subarchnoid hemorrhage. When major venous drainage channels, such as the superior sagittal sinus or the lateral sinus, are occluded, the headache results from increased intracranial pressure; it is diffuse, worse with postural changes and straining, and frequently associated with papilledema and obtundation. Venous infarction of the parenchyma may produce focal deficits such as leg weakness or hemiparesis. When the cavernous sinus is involved, the headache tends to be, in the early stages, unilateral and retro-ocular; typically it is associated with proptosis and chemosis of the eye and evidence of dysfunction of the third or sixth cranial nerve (diplopia). When intracranial venous occlusion is suspected clinically, immediate referral to a specialist is necessary.

While angiography remains the diagnostic gold standard, CT scanning may show multifocal changes in parenchyma, cerebral edema, and evidence of venous sinus occlusion; magnetic resonance imaging (MRI) with venography (MRV) is quickly becoming the procedure of choice. Heparin, followed by warfarin, is the accepted therapy, and thrombolysis by catheter instillation of urokinase directly into the occluded venous channel is under trial.

Arterial Dissection

Arterial dissection is another uncommon entity that, when it occurs, is nearly always accompanied by pain—sometimes in the head, sometimes the neck, sometimes both—and a neurologic deficit. Dissection (burrowing of blood from the lumen into the wall of a cervical or cranial artery) may be spontaneous (with no evident cause), may occur in a region of pre-existing fibromuscular dysplasia, or may follow trauma to the head or neck. Though any kind of trauma may produce dissection, typically the injury is a twisting one, such as occurs in assaults, contact sports (e.g., football tackles around the neck), and chiropractic manipulation. Pain results from distortion and tearing of the vessel wall; the neurologic deficit results from occlusion of the lumen from either the bulk of the intramural hemorrhage, or embolization of thrombus from the flap of torn intima. Any vessel may dissect: most often affected is the internal carotid artery just below the skull base, but dissection of vertebral, middle cerebral and basilar arteries have all been described. With dissection of the internal carotid artery, the periarterial sympathetic plexus may be involved, producing a Horner's syndrome.

The head and neck pain, typically, is unilateral, ipsilateral to the dissection, and severe. It lasts from several days to a few weeks and may present with headache in isolation. However, neurologic deficits resulting from infarction of the cerebral hemisphere or brain stem usually follow the onset of the pain within hours or days. Suspect dissection when there is the subacute onset of a new, unilateral severe head, neck or facial pain. Look for a Horner's syndrome, and listen for a carotid or intracranial bruit, but be aware that these are absent in over one-half of the proven cases. Immediate referral to a neurologist is prudent.

Doppler studies may increase the degree of suspicion of dissection, but angiography is necessary to either establish or rule out the presence of arterial dissection. Recently MRI with magnetic resonance angiography has shown promise in making a noninvasive diagnosis.

The treatment of arterial dissection is controversial: most neurologists will begin anticoagulation in an attempt to prevent embolization of thrombus from the intimal flap.

Atherosclerotic and Embolic Cerebrovascular Ischemic Disease

Atherosclerotic and embolic cerebrovascular ischemic disease is extremely common, particularly in the elderly. Between 25 and 50% of patients with strokes or transient ischemic attacks develop new headaches, often days or weeks before the deficit occurs. Because this is not widely appreciated, an opportunity to prevent strokes is lost.

The mechanism of these headaches is mysterious. They are not due to distention of collateral circulation, for they may occur in people with no angiographic evidence of collateral flow. It may be that amines liberated from platelet-fibrin thrombi are wafted downstream, causing chemically-induced vasodilatation. Whatever their cause, the headaches have the characteristics of vascular headaches: they are unilateral, more often than not; they can be throbbing, especially when the patient exerts; they typically last hours; and they are more likely to occur in people who had migraine when they were younger.

There is nothing specific about them. Given, however, that the onset of migraine or other "benign dysfunctional headaches" such as tension-type headaches for the first time after the age of 50 years is rare, the appearance of new headache in the elderly should prompt consideration of ingravescent stroke, a search for stroke risk factors, and early referral. Though somewhat inelegantly ad hoc, starting such patients on daily acetylsalicylic acid until their new onset headaches can be sorted out has the merits of prudence and practicality.

CRITICAL DECISIONS IN CEREBROVASCULAR HEADACHES

People with headaches due to cerebrovascular disease seldom have long histories because the underlying illness, unless recognized and treated, usually does not permit a prolonged clinical course. The physician, therefore, is confronted with a patient with headaches of recent onset, and from that starting point has to make a number of critical decisions.

Do these headaches sound like migraine or tension-type headaches? There is seldom much difficulty deciding this. Benign dysfunctional headaches present a long history of fairly stereotypical episodes, sometimes with characteristic accompaniments, in a patient who is quite well between attacks; this is not so with most cerebrovascular headaches, which are variable in "morphology," often nondescript, and which occur in patients who, generally speaking, are systemically ill and manifest this (when asked) through other complaints.

Is anything about the patient atypical for migraine or tension-type headache? Age is an obvious signal of something suspicious; benign headaches seldom commence for the first time after early middle age, but atherothrombotic vascular disease, temporal (giant cell) arteritis, and brain hemorrhage typically have an onset from 50 years of age and beyond. Pregnancy is another warning signal. Migraine can occur for the first time during pregnancy, but not often; in this situation it is prudent to think about problems such as hypertension (eclampsia), intracranial venous thrombosis, and even dissection.

Is the physical examination, including the neurologic, normal? This is a key question. All the cerebrovascular diseases discussed in this chapter can, and most often do, display abnormal physical signs. Subarachnoid hemorrhage usually is associated with signs of meningeal irritation, though sometimes they have to be carefully sought out. Parenchymal brain hemorrhage produces blatant focal signs such as hemiparesis, and often obtundation. Though high blood pressure may be an incidental finding in patients with benign headaches, its presence should prompt some thought. Patients with the commoner forms of vasculitis may have signs of vascular disease or of involvement of other organs. Intracranial venous occlusion is often associated with papilledema, focal deficits, and evidence of underlying disease. Arterial dissections may display neck or cranial bruits or a Horner's syndrome. People with headaches due to atherosclerotic and embolic cerebrovascular ischemic disease nearly always are loaded with signs of cardiovascular disease. Remember, though—if you don't look, you don't find.

A LITTLE REASSURANCE

The thought that there are several potentially lethal vascular diseases that can present as headaches is scary. But, deciding the issues discussed in this chapter should substantially reduce the risk of making a catastrophic error. To summarize a few key points:

- It is rare for vascular diseases to produce headaches which *exactly* mimic migraine or other benign dysfunctional headaches; thus, if there are *any* unusual features about the headache, *investigate*.
- Few of these vascular diseases produce headaches that walk alone; sometimes blatantly (as in parenchymal brain hemorrhage and intracranial veno-occlusive disease), sometimes subtly (as in dissection and vasculitis), symptoms or signs of vascular or neurologic disease accompany the headache. If you think to *look for them*, you will likely see them.
- Benign dysfunctional headaches such as migraine, tension-type headache, and cluster headache begin before middle age; headaches beginning for the first time *after middle age* are due to disease until proven otherwise.
- *If in doubt, refer.*

Critical Decisions

A Optional imaging
- May be done if patient unusually old for most of benign dysfunctional headaches (i.e., > 35 years).

B Lumbar puncture for worst headache ever
- Absolutely necessary if CT fails to show the cause of headache.
- CT may be normal in 10–15% of all subarachnoid hemorrhage.

C Use CT, not MRI for fulminating onset headache
- MRI may miss fresh blood.

D Symptomatic management
- Includes supervised analgesics and use of physical methods (e.g., heat, relaxation).

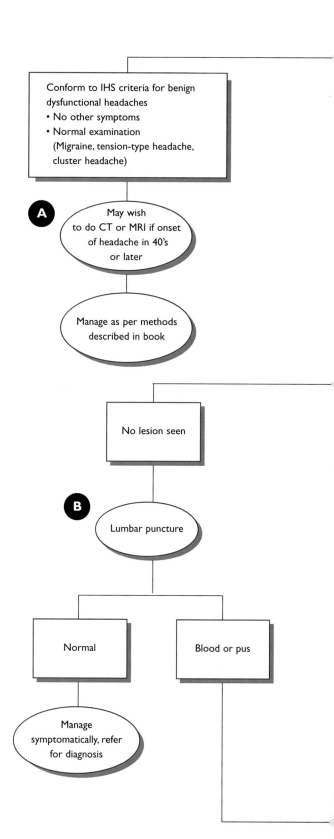

Cerebrovascular Headaches

Headaches of recent onset

Do not conform to IHS criteria for benign dysfunctional headaches
• May have other symptoms
• May have abnormal examination(Cerebrovascular lesions, mass lesions, inflammation)

Fulminant onset; "the worst headache ever" (Subarachnoid hemorrhage, intracerebral hemorrhage, meningitis)

Subacutely evolving headache (arterial dissection, vasculitis, veno-occlusive disease, brain tumor, intracranial hypertension, atherosclerotic or embolic cerebrovascular disease)

C CT scan

CT or MRI scan

Lesion identified

Lesion identified

No lesion seen

Doppler, cardiac echo, angiitis workup, lumbar puncture, angiography

Lesion identified

All normal

D Manage symptomatically and refer for diagnosis

Specific management of identified problem (usually involves referral to appropriate specialist)

Bibliography

Ameri A, Bousser MG. Cerebral venous thrombosis. In: Olesen J, Tfelt-Hanson P, Welch KMA, eds. The headaches. New York: Raven Press, 1993:671–673.

Arboix A, Massons J, Oliveres M, et al. Headache in acute cerebrovascular disease—a prospective clinical study in 240 patients. Cephalalgia 1994; 14:37–40.

Bengtsson BA, Malmvall BE. Giant cell arteritis. Acta Medica Scand 1982; (Suppl 658): 1–102.

Biousse V, D'Anglejan-Chatillon J, Massiou H, Bousser MG. Head pain in non-traumatic carotid dissection—a series of 65 patients. Cephalalgia 1994; 14:33–36.

Calabrese LH, Mallek JA. Primary angiitis of the central nervous system. Report of eight new cases, review of the literature, and proposal for diagnostic criteria. Medicine 1987; 67:20–39.

DeBruijn SFTM, Stam J, Kapelle LI. For the CVST Study Group. Thunderclap headache as the first symtom of cerebral venous sinus thrombosis. Lancet: 348; 1623–1625.

Edmeads J. Headache in cerebrovascular disease. In: Rose FC, ed. Handbook of clinical neurology, Vol 4 (48): Headache. Amsterdam: Elsevier Science Publishers, 1986:273–290.

Kase C, Williams JP, Wyatt DA, Mohr JP. Lobar intracerebral hematomas: a clinical and CT analysis of 22 cases. Neurology 1982; 32:1146–1150.

Sturzenegger M. Head and neck pain—the warning symptoms of vertebral artery dissection. Headache 1994; 34:187–193.

Vestergaard K, Andersen MD, Nielsen MI, Jensen TS. Headache in stroke. Stroke 1994; 24:1621–1624.

Weir B. Headaches from aneurysms. Cephalalgia 1994; 14:79–87.

Supplementary Search Strategies

SuSS 1

Subject	explode Headache (index term) or headache (text word)
Subject	explode Cerebrovascular Disorders (index term)
Subject	Diagnosis
Limited to	1994 through 1997

SuSS 2

Subject	explode Headache (index term)) or headache (text word)
Subject	Cerebrovascular Disorders (index term)
Limited to	Meta-Analysis (publication type) or Clinical Trial (publication type)
AND	1994 through 1997

SuSS 3

Subject	explode Headache (index term) or headache (text word)
Subject	explode Hypertension (index term)
Limited to	1994 through 1997

Chapter 14

Medication-Induced Headaches

WHAT ARE THEY?

The headache sufferer who consumes medication for acute attacks on a regular, repeated and predictable basis is at risk of developing chronic daily headaches that are caused by that medication. Migraine patients are more likely than those with tension-type headaches or cluster headaches to experience this problem. While any "acute medication" taken too regularly can produce these "medication-induced" or "rebound" headaches, those particularly likely to do so are analgesics (ASA or acetaminophen) combined with an opiate (codeine) and/or a barbiturate (butal-bital), and ergotamine tartrate. Overly frequent doses of acetaminophen or ASA with caffeine also may cause rebound headaches. There is some debate as to whether plain ASA or acetaminophen induce headaches—we think they can.

Why and how they occur is uncertain, but it is likely that the receptors of migraine patients in particular become keenly attuned to the cyclic decreases in drug levels that occur between regular doses of analgesic or ergotamine, and develop a withdrawal or rebound response to them which results in headache; certainly, boosting the drug levels with another dose will reduce or remove the headache—until that dose wears off.

Though only recently recognized as an entity, medication-induced headaches are now acknowledged to be epidemic.

CLINICAL RECOGNITION

Typically, the patient is a migraine sufferer who goes on, after some years of fairly widely spaced attacks, to develop increasingly frequent episodes which culminate in chronic daily headaches. These chronic headaches lose some of their migrainous features as they evolve, and come to resemble a mix between migraine without aura and tension-type headaches. They are seldom purely hemicranial, seldom severe, and seldom accompanied by vomiting; but they may throb, they may be associated with mild nausea, and they tend to wear the patient down with their regular and predictable recurrence. The more analgesic or ergotamine the patient takes, the less well it works and the more it is "needed." The patient's worst nightmare is being caught without medication; this will result in headaches of great severity, which can then assume the characteristics of a more typical migraine attack with vomiting and prostration. Migraine prophylactic medications prove useless in preventing medication-induced headaches; only the offending medications, taken pre-emptively ("because I know I'll get a headache if I don't") will even partially avert headaches, and so the patients cling increasingly tenaciously to their pills. Often patients are depressed, and experience sleep disturbances (particularly early morning awakening), difficulty in concentrating, restlessness, irritability and "low mood."

Many patients do not consider over-the-counter (OTC) drugs to be "real medications" and therefore will not volunteer that they are taking them. The physician should always ask. Probe, as persistently as necessary, to determine the precise amount of all medications taken per day or per week. A useful way to avoid ambiguity is to tell the patient, "Medication is anything you put in your mouth other than food." Though most people with medication-induced headaches take medication every day, three days of consumption per week is sufficient to set up and perpetuate rebound headaches. Though most people with this condition take in excess of 100 tablets per month, it is regularity, not quantity, that determines whether medication-induced headaches will occur.

MANAGEMENT

As with any chronic daily headache, the first step is to establish the diagnosis beyond doubt. The history of previously widely spaced migraine attacks evolving into a chronic daily pattern *pari passu* with the establishment of a regular predictable intake of analgesics or ergotamine, with a normal general physical and neurologic examination should suffice—but some patients need the reassurance of normal imaging. It is prudent to do a complete blood count (CBC) and some renal (BUN, creatinine) and liver (AST/SGOT) function studies, since over-use of medications may have produced some clinically silent problems.

Educating the patient about the role of medications in causing headaches is crucial. The use of terms such as "addicted" or "dependent" is inaccurate and counterproductive; it is preferable to talk about "receptors" and "rebound." The need to get off medication must be driven home, but at the same time there must be some assurance that the headaches which the patient dreads will be addressed. A useful thing in motivating patients is to tell them that by getting off medications they will have some weeks of discomfort punctuated by short episodes of pain, but will gain an 80% chance of losing their chronic daily headaches. Involving the family in the discussion and recruiting them to help is important.

Getting the patient to start a "headache diary" (frequency, duration, and severity of headaches; timing of attacks; medication taken and its effects) has many advantages. It will show the patient the precise number of tablets that (s)he takes (often a shock), it will demonstrate the pattern of headaches starting as the effects of a dose of medication ends, and it will serve as a baseline for measuring progress.

Once an adequate baseline has been obtained (a couple of weeks usually suffices), the medication should be stopped—abruptly. Only analgesics containing barbiturates need to be weaned; failure to do this can result in barbiturate-withdrawal seizures. Headaches inevitably follow the cessation of medication:

a) Mild or moderate headaches should not be treated with medication. Ice-packs and/or a tight band (such as a dishtowel) can be applied to the head, and the patient should "tough it out."

b) Severe headaches can be treated with the measures above, plus a good dose of an NSAID (such as sodium naproxen, two 550 mg tablets) and, if needed, an oral antinauseant such as metoclopramide 10 mg or a rectal one such as dimenhydrinate 50–100 mg.

c) Very severe headaches may require an intravenous neuroleptic such as chlorpromazine 10–25 mg, or an intravenous DHE "cocktail" (dihydroergotamine 0.75–1.0 mg with metoclopramide 10 mg), or subcutaneous sumatriptan (6 mg). Avoid narcotics!

Particularly when withdrawing from codeine-containing analgesics or barbiturate-containing analgesics, and especially if these have been consumed in large quantities, some patients may experience distressing tremulousness, anxiety, irritability, nausea, vomiting, diarrhea, muscle cramps, and other symptoms. Oral chlorpromazine, up to 75 mg per day, or clonidine 0.2 mg twice each day, are helpful in suppressing these withdrawal symptoms.

Once off the analgesic or ergotamine, the patient should be started on a migraine prophylactic agent, for these will now begin to work. Amitriptyline in a dose of 10–50 mg at night can be especially useful because it also has some intrinsic analgesic activity.

Sometimes this outpatient withdrawal program does not work, and hospital admission may be necessary. This should not be a frequent occurrence. Hospital admission will allow tight supervision of the patient and control of his or her medications, it may allow the exclusion of some friends or family members who have an adverse effect on the patient's resolve ("I hate to see you suffer so, dear—one little painkiller can't hurt you that much!"), and will allow the administration of repetitive intravenous DHE to break the cycle of rebound headaches.

To administer repetitive intravenous DHE, first ensure that there are no contraindications (hypertension, cardiovascular disease, liver or kidney problems, pregnancy). Insert a saline or heparin lock into an arm vein. There are various protocols for determining doses of DHE (see, for example, Raskin) incorporating the following principles:

a) Give an initial dose of antinauseant IV first, since intravenous DHE without this "cover" is highly likely to produce vomiting. Metoclopramide 10 mg, or prochlorperazine 5–10 mg, dissolved in 50 mL of 5% dextrose in water, and infused over 15 minutes, are good choices.

b) Then infuse a medium dose of DHE (0.5 mg) IV over about 1 minute, as a test dose.

c) If this dose causes adverse effects other than nausea (for example, chest pain, changes in blood pressure), abandon the DHE, even if it helped the headache.

d) If this dose produces severe nausea (not likely), but helps the headache, try again in 8 hours at a dose of 0.25 mg with a regular dose of antinauseant, and if this helps the headache then use that dose for maintenance (see below). If it does not help the headache, go back to 0.5 mg of DHE with a double dose of antinauseant, and use this for maintenance.

e) If this dose does not help the headache, and does not produce nausea, give another 0.5 mg of DHE intravenously right away, and if it helps the headache and does not provoke nausea, use 1.0 mg as the maintenance dose of DHE.

f) If this dose helps the headache, and does not produce nausea, use it (DHE 0.5 mg) as the maintenance dose.

g) Once the maintenance dose of DHE has been determined (usually 0.5–1.0 mg), infuse it as a cocktail with an antinauseant (prochlorperazine 5 mg or metoclopramide 5–10 mg) in 50 ml of 5% dextrose in water, every 8 hours until the headaches abate (usually 2 or 3 days); and then every 12 hours for two or three doses before discontinuing. Sometimes this "DHE regimen" needs to be continued longer. If so, outpatient treatment can be accomplished by administering DHE as a twice-daily intramuscular injection (0.5 mg bid) for up to 14 days. The patient or the family can be trained to administer the injection.

Getting the patients off their analgesics or ergotamine is usually not difficult, but *keeping* them off can be a major problem. It is essential to see them frequently (every 1 to 2 weeks) during and *after* the withdrawal process, and to be available to them on the telephone between visits. There is a high incidence of recidivism in these patients; they fall off the wagon easily unless they are given moral support by their physicans and families, and, sometimes, pharmacologic support from good doses of migraine prophylactic medications.

PREVENTION

Ensuring that headache patients do not develop medication-induced headaches is easier than unhooking them once these headaches have taken over. Some simple measures usually suffice:

1. Recognize that there is variability in attacks of migraine and other headaches; some are moderate, some are severe, and some are mild—in about that order of frequency for most people. It makes no more sense to prescribe just one medication for a patient to treat *all* of his or her attacks than it does to play a round of golf with just one club. Prescribing a specific antimigraine medication such as sumatriptan or ergotamine for mild attacks of migraine is overkill; it puts the patient at some risk and some expense when that attack could be handled by a simple analgesic. Conversely, prescribing analgesics for all headaches, including severe ones where they are foredoomed to give at best mediocre relief, puts the patient in the position of having to take more and more of this medication in search of relief, with a much greater chance of developing medication-induced headaches. Tailor your prescriptions to the patient's situation.
2. Remind the patient frequently that analgesics, ergotamine, and just about any "acute" medication can lead to rebound headaches if taken too "regularly". Encourage the patient to keep a headache diary, in which the amounts of all medication taken are recorded. Emphasize that if an "acute" medication is being taken more than three days in a week, it is being taken too often. This patient probably needs a migraine prophylactic medication.
3. Do not write renewable prescriptions for analgesics or ergotamine.

Medication-Induced Headache

A Educate patient about MIHs

B Patient starts headache diary

Overused medication contains barbiturate

Overused medication does not contain a barbiturate

C Wean off medication/start migraine prophylaxis medication

Discontinue medication abruptly/start migraine prophylactic medication

Outpatient management

Ultrasevere headache

Severe headache

Mild-to-moderate headache

Other withdrawal symptoms

IV. neuroleptic or IV DHE or SQ sumatriptan

IM DHE NSAID ± antinauseant SC sumatriptan

No medication, use local cold or pressure

Chlorpromazine or clonidine

Headaches ease

Headaches do not ease

Maintain prophylactic medication/ close follow-up

D Go to inpatient management

Critical Decisions

A
- Patient education is the first critical step in treatment.
- Stress the importance of getting off medication.
- Make patient aware that headaches may initially worsen, but should eventually improve.

B

Maintain headache diary
Headache diary includes:
- frequency of attacks
- duration of attacks
- severity of attacks
- timing of attacks
- medication taken and its effect.

C

Wean from medication
- These patients may experience tremulousness, anxiety, irritability, nausea, vomiting, diarrhea, and muscle cramps.
- Failure to wean from barbiturates may result in withdrawal seizures.

D

Inpatient management
- If withdrawal from medication on an outpatient basis is ineffective, hospitalization may be required.
- Hospitalization allows tight control of medication and close monitoring of potential withdrawal symptoms. It also permits parenteral use of medication, namely, DHE.

Repetitive I.V. DHE

Contraindicated

No contraindication

Give antinauseant IV

Test dose 0.5 mg DHE IV

Chest pain, increased BP, etc

Headache not helped

Headache helped but nauseated

Headache helped, no nausea

Abandon DHE

Give another 0.5 mg DHE stat, to bring total to 1.0 mg

Try again in 8 hr with 0.25 mg DHE and antinauseant

Headache helped, not nauseated

Headache not helped

Headache helped but nauseated

Headache helped

Headache not helped

Abandon DHE

In 8 hr, use 1.0 mg DHE with double dose of antinauseant

No nausea

Maintenance dose is 0.5 mg DHE with regular dose antinauseant

Nausea persists

No nausea

Abandon DHE

Maintenance dose is 0.25 mg DHE and antinauseant

Maintenance dose of DHE is 1.0 mg with regular antinauseant

Maintenance dose is 1.0 mg DHE with double antinauseant

Maintenance dose is 0.5 mg DHE with double antinauseant

Maintenance dose q8h IV until headaches gone (usually 2–3 days) Wean DHE by giving maintenance dose q12h for 2 or 3 doses, then discontinue

E

Keep patient on migraine prophylactic medication, deny analgesics and ergotamine, and follow-up closely.

E

Follow-up
- Maintain close follow-up during and after the withdrawal process.
- Remind patient that analgesics, ergotamine, and almost any "acute medication" can lead to rebound headache if taken too frequently.

- Encourage the use of a headache diary listing the amounts of medication taken.
- If medication is taken more than three times per week, consider preventive measures.
Note: Do *not* write renewable prescriptions for analgesics or ergotamine.

Bibiography

Edmeads J, Grenville A, Aube M. Migraine variability: an underrecognized impediment to effective treatment. Pain Res Manage 1996; 1:215–218.

Hering R, Steiner TJ. Abrupt outpatient withdrawal of medications in analgesic abusing migraineurs. Lancet 1991; 337:1442–1443.

Mathew NT. Chronic refractory headache. Neurology 1993; 43(Suppl 3):S26–S35.

Raskin NH. Repetitive intravenous dihydroergotamine as therapy for intractable migraine. Neurology 1986; 36:995–997.

Sheftell F. Chronic daily headaches. Neurology 1992; 42(Suppl 2):S32–S36.

Supplementary Search Strategy

SuSS 1	
Subject	explode Headache (index term) or headache (text word)
Subject	explode chemically-induced (subheading)
Limited to	1994 through 1997

Chapter 15

EMERGENCY MANAGEMENT OF ACUTE HEADACHE

As a primary symptom, headache accounts for 1 to 2% of emergency department visits. The majority of these patients either have an acute exacerbation of an underlying primary headache disorder, or an acute febrile illness. Nevertheless, the concern of overlooking a more sinister cause should be ever-present.

A directed evaluation, emphasizing the clinical history, is the approach most applicable for excluding disorders that can be life-threatening or disabling. The usual paucity of physical findings demands a higher degree of clinical acumen in a disorder where the history is the "gold standard" for diagnosis.

A manageable classification of headache in the emergency department will serve to sequester the serious headaches from the more "benign" recurrent headache disorders. Patients with headache should be classified into one of the following three headache categories:

• The "first, worst, or different" syndrome
• Subacute or progressive headache syndrome
• Chronic daily or recurrent-stereotyped headache syndrome.

HISTORY

As with any medical complaint, the physician must actively assess the tempo and duration of the symptom. These are arguably the most important facts of a headache history in the emergency room. The location and severity, aggravating and relieving factors, and the presence of associated systemic or neurologic features are also critical for securing an accurate diagnosis. These are reviewed in Chapter 4.

The following headache-associated features should always cause concern and warrant immediate referral and investigation:

- Abrupt onset or an unusually severe headache, particularly if associated with neurologic symptoms. A complaint that a particular headache is "different" than others previously experienced, should always be pursued
- Subacute or progressive headache over days to months
- Headache associated with nausea, vomiting, and fever not explained by systemic illness
- New onset headache in adult life (> 40 years), or a significant change of a long-standing headache problem
- Precipitation of headache with Valsalva (cough, sneeze, strain, bend) position change, head turning, exercise, and coitus
- Headaches associated with nocturnal occurrence or morning awakening
- Headaches associated with neurologic signs or symptoms such as confusion, decreased level of consciousness or cognition, meningismus, or papilledema
- Systemic symptoms such as fever, jaw claudication, weight loss, myalgias.

PHYSICAL EXAMINATION

Most of the errors made in headache diagnosis can be traced to an inadequate history. This should not undermine the importance of a careful and thoughtful physical examination as only half an opinion can be given in its absence. The physical examination of a headache patient should, as a minimum, evaluate:

- Vital signs (blood pressure, heart rate, temperature)
- Cardiac status
- Extracranial structures (sinuses, scalp arteries, paraspinal muscles, temporo-mandibular joints) for tenderness
- Range of motion and the presence of pain in the cervical spine.

A screening neurologic examination capable of detecting most of the abnormal signs likely to occur in patients with headaches due to intracranial or systemic disease should be performed. This should include the following:

- Neck flexion (for evidence of meningeal irritation)
- The presence of bruits over the cranium, orbits, or neck
- The optic fundi, visual fields, pupillary reactions, fifth cranial nerve sensory function and corneal reflexes, motor power in the face and limbs, muscle stretch reflexes and gait.

INVESTIGATIONS

General Tests

A complete blood count (CBC) with a differential, chemistry profile, and a sedimentation rate should be part of every headache evaluation. These baseline laboratory parameters will help to exclude systemic causes as well as serve as a template for comparison prior to initiating a medication regimen. Other tests (C-spine films, sinus x-rays, chest x-ray) will of course be dictated by the historical and physical examination findings.

Neuroimaging

A computed tomography (CT) scan is the imaging modality of choice for a headache evaluation in the emergency room. It is more accessible, less costly, and more sensitive than magnetic resonance imaging (MRI) for detecting acute subarachnoid blood. The diagnostic yield in patients with subarachnoid hemorrhage (SAH) exceeds 95% initially, but the sensitivity is time dependent, falling to 50% at day 7, and at day 10, a CT will rarely detect blood in a patient who presents with a sentinel bleed.

Important causes of headache that are often overlooked on an unenhanced CT (Figure 15.1)and may require MRI, lumbar puncture, or a systemic evaluation, include:

- Cortical or dural venous sinus thrombosis
- Posterior fossa lesions
- Diffuse infiltrative glioma
- Primary or secondary CNS vasculitis
- Idiopathic intracranial hypertension
- Meningitis (or leptomeningeal involvement) and encephalitis
- Sphenoid sinusitis ("sinus CT")
- Temporal arteritis
- Arterial dissection

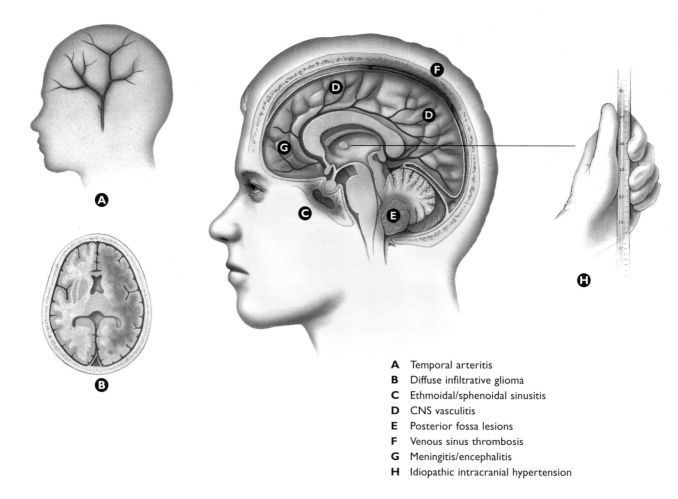

A Temporal arteritis
B Diffuse infiltrative glioma
C Ethmoidal/sphenoidal sinusitis
D CNS vasculitis
E Posterior fossa lesions
F Venous sinus thrombosis
G Meningitis/encephalitis
H Idiopathic intracranial hypertension

Figure 15.1   Causes of Headache Overlooked on an Unenhanced CT Scan

Lumbar Puncture

After the neurologic examination and neuroimaging tests fail to uncover the cause, a cerebrospinal fluid (CSF) examination is mandatory in patients who present with:

- The first, worst, or unusually severe headache
- A severe rapid onset, recurrent headache
- A subacute/progressive headache
- An atypical chronic intractable headache
- A headache associated with fever.

Some caveats regarding lumbar puncture (LP):

- If the CSF is negative within 6 hours of headache onset in a patient with a suspected SAH and normal CT, repeat the LP. (Sufficient time is required to elapse for subarachnoid blood to sediment down to the lumbar thecal space.)
- If a traumatic tap is suspected, unless an unequivocal decrease in red blood cell count is seen between the first and final sample, a spectrophotometric analysis is the most reliable method of detecting hemolyzed red cell products (oxyhemoglobin and bilirubin) because of their characteristic spectral peaks, confirming an SAH.
- Despite the progressive time-dependent decline in CT sensitivity for subarachnoid blood, xanthachromia should persist for approximately 14 days after a sentinel bleed.
- Always measure opening pressure, since this may be the first manifestation of raised intracranial pressure, often present in patients with SAH or meningitis.
- If bacterial meningitis is suspected, do not delay lumbar puncture until after a CT scan is done if focal neurologic findings are absent; tap and treat immediately. If you are reluctant to do an LP, start antibiotics without LP, since hypoglycorrhachia will persist for three days, the pleocytosis and protein elevation will be present up to 10 days later and the infectious disease specialist can clean up after you by identifying common organisms with serologic tests.

TREATMENT IN THE EMERGENCY SETTING

When a specific disorder is revealed by the clinical survey, analgesics and most importantly, directed treatment, should be given.

Fortunately, a majority of headaches in the emergency setting will not be secondary to serious systemic or intracranial disease. Most patients will have chronic daily or recurrent primary headache syndromes. Unfortunately, a minority of patients in this category appear hypochondriacal and manipulative and often have significant medication problems such as drug dependence (both emotionally and physiologically), drug-seeking behavior, and analgesic-rebound (medication-induced) headaches. The latter group of patients usually at one point have a recurrent primary headache disorder (migraine or tension-type headache), which innocently transforms into a chronic daily headache as their consumption of analgesics containing codeine, barbiturate, caffeine, or ergotamine increased in response to an increase in headache frequency.

Critical Decisions

A. Thunderclap headaches
- Explosive and severe headache with hyperacute onset.
- Normal physical examination.
- May signal possibility of subarachnoid hemorrhage— CT without contrast.
- 5–10% of CT scans do not reveal subarachnoid blood or hemorrhage is subtle and overlooked.

B. Lumbar puncture
- If CT scan is negative, patients with thunderclap headaches should have lumbar puncture because of the small false-negative rate with CT scans in detecting SAH.
- Analyze CSF for blood and its breakdown product, xanthachromia, cells, protein, glucose, and opening pressure.
- Analyze serum glucose and protein to properly evaluate the CSF/serum ratios to detect relative abnormalities.

C. Magnetic resonance imaging
- Should be done when neurologic signs/symptoms persist despite normal LP and CT.
- Serious abnormalities that may not be obvious on CT or LP include pituitary apoplexy, cerebral venous sinus thrombosis, encephalitis, and CNS vasculitis.

D. Subacute/progressive headaches
- All subacute and new onset progressive headaches require urgent attention and evaluation.
- ESR is mandatory in patients over age 50 presenting with a new headache to rule out the possibility of temporal arteritis.
- See Chapter 4, *History and Physical Examination,* for an outline of the signs and symptoms which should raise suspicion about an underlying systemic or intracranial process.

E. Imaging subacute headaches
- In the absence of systemic or metabolic cause for headaches, CT should be performed to rule out an obvious intracranial process.
- If CT is negative, an opening CSF pressure and CSF analysis should be performed, and MRI with contrast is necessary to exclude idiopathic intracranial hypertension, cerebral venous sinus thrombosis, leptomeningeal syndromes, or infiltrative neoplasm.

Red Flag Headaches

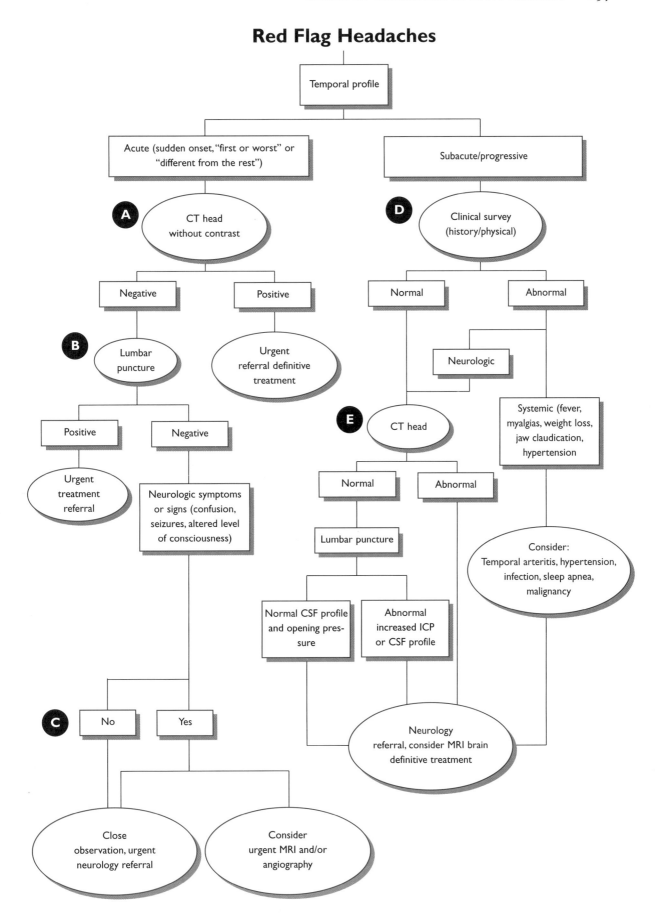

Critical Decisions

 Oral NSAID
- Ibuprofen 400–800 mg PO
- ASA (buffered or soluble) 650–1300 mg PO
- Naproxen 275–550 mg PO
- Ketoprofen 100 mg PO

B
- Sumatriptan (Imitrex) 6 mg SQ or 25–100 mg PO

C DHE
- Metoclopramide (Reglan) 10 mg IV push.
- DHE 0.5–1.0 mg IV/IM—may repeat q60 min. to max of 2 mg IV or 3 mg IM per attack, or 6 mg/week. May be given as IV push over 2–3 min. or diluted in 50 mL of normal saline IV over 15–30 min. For subsequent visits, the total effective dose can be given as a single injection.

D Neuroleptics
- To avoid hypertension, pretreat with 500–1000 mL IV normal saline bolus before administering neuroleptics.
- Prochlorperazine (Compazine/Stemetil) 5–10 mg IV (max IV concentration 1 mg/mL; maximum rate of 1 mg/min)
- Chlorpromazine (Thorazine/Largactil) 5 mg IVq5 min. until headache clears, or a maximum of 25 mg given

E Parenteral NSAID or narcotic
- Parenteral NSAID: ketorolac (Toradol) 30–60 mg as a single IM injection
- Parenteral narcotic: meperidine (Demerol) 75–100 mg IM/IV plus antiemetic

F Parenteral corticosteroid
- Dexamethasone 12–20 IM/IV
- Hydrocortisone IV 100–250 mg
- A repeat parenteral or its oral equivalent may be given within 24 hours.

Acute Migraine Treatment

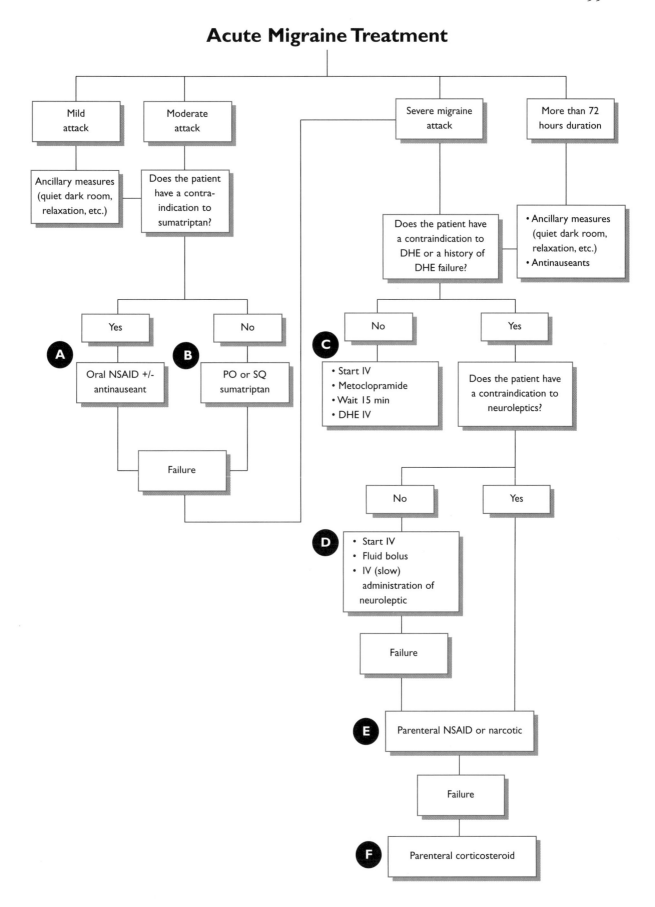

It is both unrealistic and inappropriate for the emergency room physician to provide a definitive management program for such chronic, convoluted, and complex headache disorders. Based upon the patient's previous headache history, referral to a pain management or headache program for detoxification, or admission to a primary medical or neurologic hospital service for analgesic withdrawal and headache management is most appropriate. Analgesic prescriptions or parenteral narcotics will provide a "quick fix," but will only perpetuate the problem and ensure the patient's swift return.

For a majority of patients, emergency room treatment will suffice for the acute headache, but an outpatient appointment with either the primary physician or a neurologist should be arranged to establish a more comprehensive and definitive long-term preventive and symptomatic treatment program.

Simple analgesics have often failed (almost by definition) in those patients who present to the emergency department for pain relief. While individual physician approaches may vary with respect to the sequence and/or combination of agents used, all are variations upon a theme. The following are treatment options for the primary headache disorders which most often frequent the emergency room.

Migraine

Most migraineurs who appear in the emergency room do so because the usual abortive agents have failed, or because they are experiencing a particularly severe or protracted headache with significant gastrointestinal symptoms. Providing a quiet, dark, and relaxing environment conducive to sleep, if possible, is optimal.

Initiating therapy with a gastric motility agent such as metoclopramide will alleviate nausea and vomiting, enhance absorption of specific antimigraine agents, and potentiate the effect of other analgesics.

Further treatment is then determined by the duration and severity of the attack, and whether it is associated with nausea, vomiting, and dehydration.

Cluster Headache

Acute attacks of cluster headache are of rapid onset and brief duration (30 to 120 minutes). The therapeutic principle, therefore, is to administer agents which provide immediate relief (see Chapter 9). Cluster patients do not frequent the ER except in the circumstance of a protracted attack or multiple daily attacks.

The most effective agents are oxygen inhalation and subcutaneous sumatriptan.

1. *Oxygen inhalation (7 liters per minute for 15 minutes using a facial mask)*
   Approximately 60 to 70% respond within 15 minutes, but a significant number may experience recurrent headache.
2. *Subcutaneous sumatriptan (6 mg)*
   Response rates range from 76 to 96% within 15 minutes, with more than one-third being pain-free within 10 minutes. Sumatriptan is well tolerated and thus far shows no evidence of tachyphylaxis or adverse events with long-term use. Severe or uncontrolled hypertension and prior myocardial ischemia are contraindications to its use.
3. *Intravenous (0.5 to 1.0 mg) or nasal (1.0 to 2.0 mg) dihydroergotamine*
4. *Intranasal lidocaine (1 cc of 4% lidocaine)*
   Applied into the nostril ipsilateral to the headache; repeat in 15 minutes, if needed. Apply in supine position, with head extended below horizontal, and painful side turned toward the floor.
5. *Prednisone 60 mg per day for 3 days*
   Followed with a dosage decrement of 10 mg every 3 days (18-day course)

Although traditionally considered a prophylactic agent, initiating corticosteroids in the emergency room may be useful in terminating a cluster cycle in conjunction with an appropriate preventive regimen initiated on an outpatient basis. Prednisone is widely held to be a very useful agent in cluster headache, but documentation in the literature is limited. Treatment should be given only after careful consideration of side effects and contraindications.

Oral or rectal ergotamine tartrate in general has limited value in the acute treatment of cluster attacks because of the delayed onset of action.

Status Migrainosus

Status migrainosus is defined under the International Headache Society (IHS) criteria as an attack of migraine, the headache phase of which lasts longer than 72 hours, with or without treatment (Headache Classification Committee of the IHS). The headache is either continuous, or headache-free intervals last less than four hours. A protocol using IV DHE and metoclopramide has gained widespread popularity and is often the method of choice employed for persistent intractable migraine. Neuroleptics are also very useful for terminating an intractable migraine attack. (See Chapter 8, *Migraine,* for details on other treatments.)

The use of corticosteroids as an effective treatment is anecdotal. The rationale for their use is uncertain, but they may reduce perivascular inflammation or sensitize the blood vessels to the vasoconstricting effect of circulating catecholamines and adjunctive migraine therapy. Hydrocortisone IV at a dose of 100 to 250 mg or dexamethasone (12 to 20 mg) IM or IV have been used. A repeat parenteral dose or its oral equivalent can be given within 24 hours. The use of corticosteroids should be considered as a treatment of last resort and initiated only after careful consideration of the risks as they pertain to each individual.

Bibliography

Bell R, Montoya D, et al. A comparative trial of three agents in the treatment of acute migraine headache. Ann Emerg Med 1990; 19:1079–1082.

Campbell JK, Zagami A. Status migrainosus. In: Oleson J, Tfelt-Hanson P, Welch KMA, eds. The headaches. New York: Raven Press, 1993:405–407.

Coppola M, et al. Randomized placebo-controlled evaluation of prochlorperazine versus metaclo-pramide for emergency department of migraine headache. Ann Emerg Med 1995; 26:541–546.

Edmeads J. Emergency management of headache. Headache 1988; 28:675–679.

Ekbom K. Treatment of cluster headache: clinical trials, design, and results. Cephalalgia 1995; 15:33–36.

Ferrari M. Sumatriptan international study group: treatment of acute migraine attacks with sumatriptan. New Engl J Med 1991; 325:316–321.

Fisher HF. A new approach to emergency department therapy of migraine headache with intra-venous haloperidol: a case series. J Emerg Med 1995; 13:119.

Headache Classification Committee of the IHS. Classification and diagnosis criteria for headache disorders, cranial neuralgias and facial pain. Cephalalgia 1988; 8(7):1–96.

Lane PL, Ross R. Intravenous chlorpromazine: preliminary results in acute migraine. Headache 1985; 25(6):302–304.

Raskin NH. Treatment of status migrainosus: the American experience. Headache 1990; 30(suppl 2):360–365.

Saadah HA. Abortive headache therapy in the office with intravenous dihydroergotamine plus prochlorperazine. Headache 1993; 32:143–146.

Silberstein SD. Evaluation and emergency treatment of headache. Headache 1992;32:396–407.

Supplementary Search Strategies

SuSS 1

Subject	explode Headache (index term) or headache (text word)
Subject	explode Emergency Medical Services (index term) or emergency (text word) or urgent (text word)
Limited to	1994 through 1997

SuSS 2

Subject	explode Headache (index term) or headache (text word)
Subject	Subarachnoid Hemorrage (index term))
Limited to	1994 through 1997

Chapter 16

HEADACHE IN CHILDREN

Headache may be the initial manifestation of central nervous system disease or an accompanying symptom of systemic illness, including respiratory or systemic infection or metabolic abnormalities. Most frequently, however, migraine or tension-headache is the cause. Because headache affects the child and his or her parents and can result in time lost from school, early recognition and treatment are important.

HISTORY AND PHYSICAL EXAMINATION

A thorough history is the key to making an accurate diagnosis. Key features of the history enable the clinician to distinguish between benign and sinister headaches. In addition to questions of duration, frequency, location, and exacerbating features, specific questions pertaining to symptoms of central nervous system disease should be addressed. These symptoms include ataxia, lethargy, fever, cognitive changes, and other aspects in the functional neurologic inquiry. New or increased headache with focal neurologic signs (e.g., hemiparesis) require an urgent CT scan and referral to a specialist.

The importance of a careful physical examination to uncover secondary causes cannot be overstated. Routine vital signs including blood pressure should be checked for abnormalities. Organ systems are evaluated; this would include inspection of the skin for abnormalities such as bruising, petechiae, and café au lait spots suggesting evidence of associated neurologic disease. In the pediatric population, head circumference should be measured for enlargement as a result of hydrocephalus or brain tumor. Cranial bruits or localized tenderness of the scalp may reveal an underlying vascular malformation or trauma. The standard neurologic examination should, as a minimum, scritinize for localized cranial nerve abnormalities, papilledema, ataxia, or focal motor or sensory findings.

REFERRAL

Referral of the child with headache should be considered if the family physician's history or physical examination raises the suspicion of neurologic or systemic disease. A diagnosis of meningitis in a child with lethargy, fever, and headache is an urgent situation that warrants immediate referral and treatment. As in the adult population, referral is recommended if the history suggests an escalation in the frequency or severity of the headache or a change in the usual pattern. Focal neurologic signs that suggest central nervous system pathology also require further workup.

In some situations referral may be for no other reason than to reassure parents and to intervene when headaches are causing lost time from school. (For patients in whom the history and physical examination do not suggest underlying pathology or systemic disease, consideration may be given to a diagnosis of depression or family dysfunction, and appropriate consultation services may be sought.)

Depending on the differential diagnosis, routine laboratory tests are the initial phase of investigation after the history and physical examination. With CT and MRI available, skull radiographs and EEGs are rarely required for investigating headache. As in the adult, CT scan should be considered if there is an unexplained increase in the frequency or severity of the headache or if there is a change in the usual pattern. Treatment-resistant headache, associated neurologic signs and symptoms, or a change in personality, also indicate the need for a CT or MRI scan. Further radiologic workup is required if there is a history of failure to grow, cognitive decline, or increase in head circumference. (See Chapter 3, *Practical Pathophysiology of Headaches* for further guidelines regarding the use of CT and MRI scanning.)

In cases in which meningitis or pseudotumor is suspected, lumbar puncture is the investigation of choice. If a mass lesion is suspected, a CT scan should be performed prior to a lumbar puncture in order to rule out mass effect.

Although reassurance and mild analgesia in most cases are all that is required for treatment of childhood headache, a trial of antimigraine therapy may be needed if the child does not respond to simple measures or if he or she is missing time from school.

The standard principles of avoiding of triggers as first-line therapy still apply. A useful exercise for the child and parents is the initiation of a "headache diary," in which headache characteristics, food intake, weather changes, and associated stress are documented. The diary should be reviewed at subsequent appointments with the child and parents.

Table 16.1 Treatment of Migraine in Children (for children >8yrs)

Drug	Route	Dosage	Major Side Effects
Abortive			
Ergotamine	Rectal/Sublingual	1–2 mg May repeat in 20 minutes; not to exceed 4 mg in 24 hours	Gastric upset
Cafergot	Oral	One tablet/1mg	Gastric upset
Prophylactic			
Propranolol	Oral (Under 14 years)	Initial dose 10 mg b.i.d. May increase by 10 mg per day each week to maximum 20 mg t.i.d.	Hypotension Provocation of underlying asthma
	(Over 14 years)	(See Table 1 in Chapter 8, *Migraine*)	
Amitriptyline	Oral	10 mg per day at bedtime May be increased by 10 mg per day each week to maximum 50 mg	Drowsiness Difficulty with concentration Dry mouth (See Chapter 8, *Migraine*, for further details.)

Analgesia (i.e., acetaminophen) may be the initial phase of medical management. Medication should be made readily available to the child, and it should be taken early in the course of the headache.

Ergotamine, prescribed to be taken sublingually or in oral tablets, may also be used as an abortive treatment. Although sumatriptan is an effective agent in the treatment of adult migraine, its effectiveness in children is still unproven.

A variety of preventive medications may be used if headaches are frequent or severe enough to be disruptive to the child's school or home life (Table 16.1).

METABOLIC ENCEPHALOPATHY WITH LACTIC ACIDOSIS AND STROKE-LIKE EPISODES (MELAS)

MELAS may present initially with vascular-type headaches associated with stroke-like symptoms. There may be associated seizures as well. The diagnosis is based on the clinical picture and the associated radiologic findings of cerebral infarction, edema, or hemorrhage. Cerebrospinal fluid demonstrates lactic and pyruvic acidosis, and the diagnosis is confirmed on muscle biopsy where ragged red and/or cytochrome oxidase negative fibers are seen.

Headache in Children and Adolescents

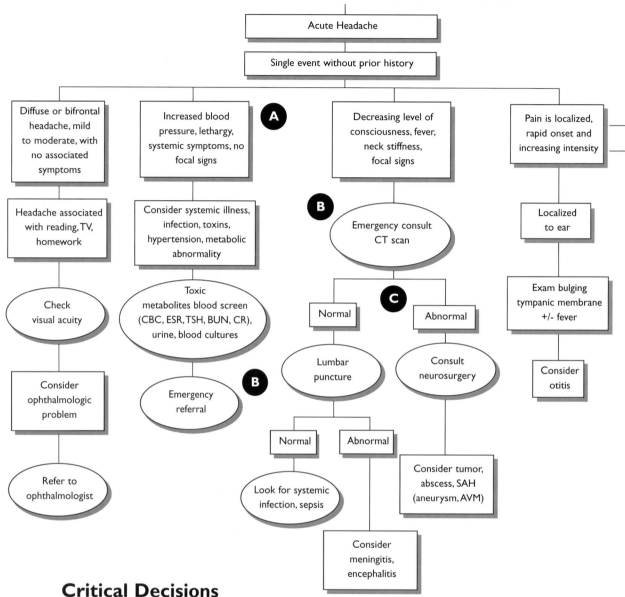

Critical Decisions

A Examination
- Examination should include head circumference, cranial bruits, localized tenderness.

B Referral necessary when:
- Headache is worsening
- Suspicion of lesion
- Focal neurologic signs
- Immediate referral for suspected meningitis (fever, headache, neck stiffness).

C Consider CT
- When situation suggests the possibility of lesion

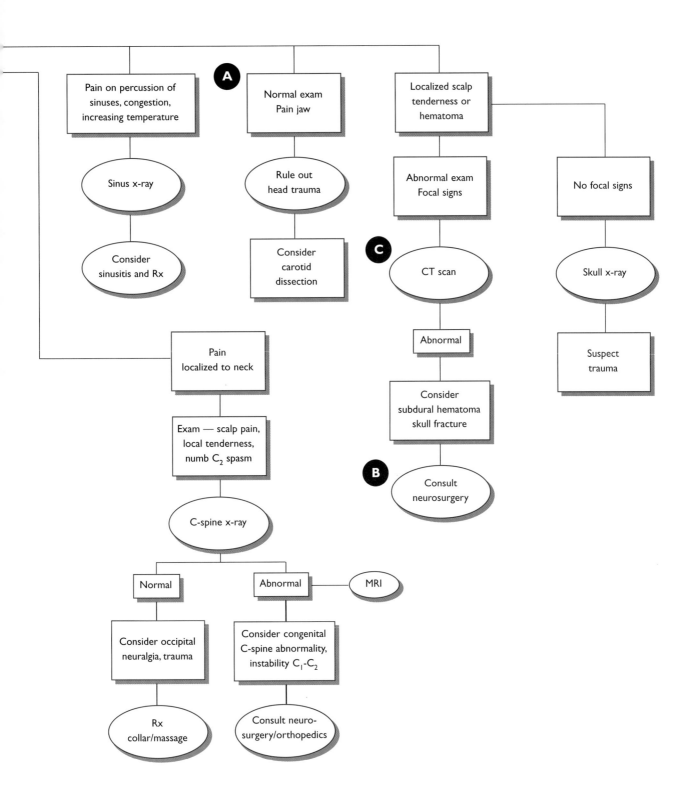

A

Pain on percussion of sinuses, congestion, increasing temperature

Sinus x-ray

Consider sinusitis and Rx

Normal exam Pain jaw

Rule out head trauma

Consider carotid dissection

Localized scalp tenderness or hematoma

Abnormal exam Focal signs

C

CT scan

Abnormal

Consider subdural hematoma skull fracture

B

Consult neurosurgery

No focal signs

Skull x-ray

Suspect trauma

Pain localized to neck

Exam — scalp pain, local tenderness, numb C_2 spasm

C-spine x-ray

Normal

Consider occipital neuralgia, trauma

Rx collar/massage

Abnormal

MRI

Consider congenital C-spine abnormality, instability C_1-C_2

Consult neuro-surgery/orthopedics

Recurrent Headache in Children and Adolescents

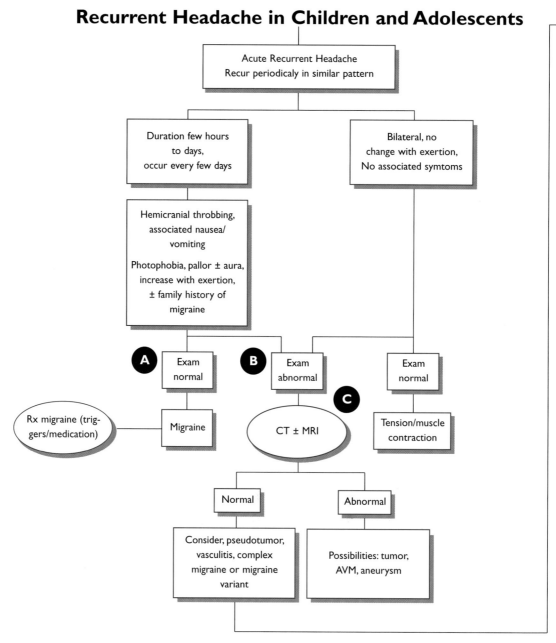

Critical Decisions

A Examination
- Examination should include head circumference, cranial bruits, localized tenderness.

B Referral suggested for:
- History suggests escalation in frequency or severity, or a change in usual pattern.
- Focal neurologic signs.
- Immediate referral for suspected meningitis (fever, headache, neck stiffness).

C Consider CT
- If headache pattern changes or headaches increase in frequency or severity.
- If headaches are resistant to treatment.
- In cases of cognitive decline, or failure to grow.

D MELAS
- MELAS (mitochondrial encephalopathy with lactic acidosis and stroke-like episodes) may initially present with vascular headache and stroke-like symptoms..

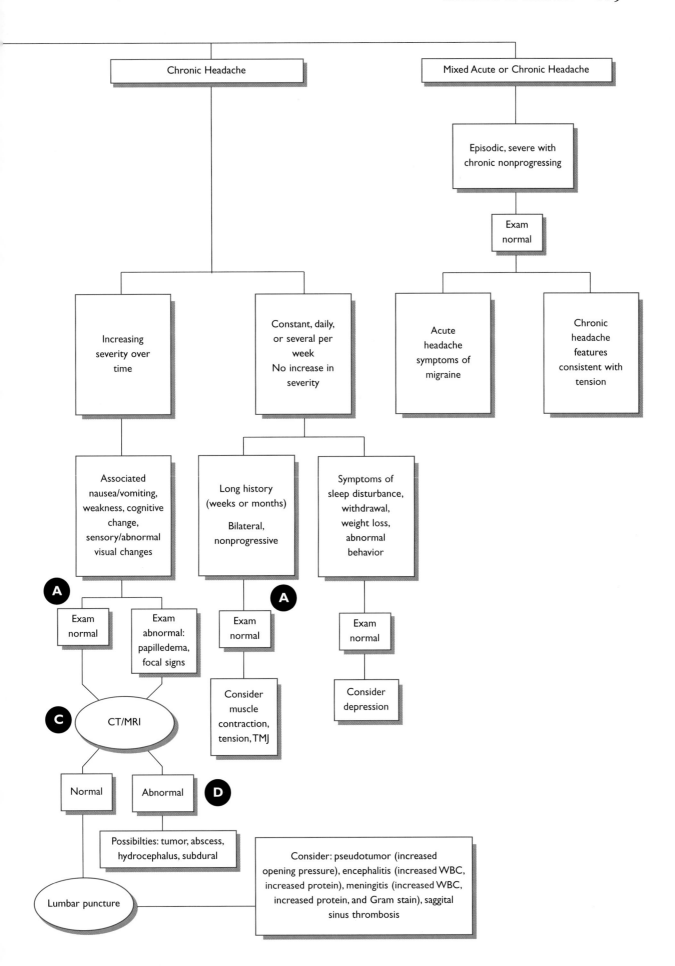

Bibliography

Fenichel GM. Migraine in children. In: (eds) Neurologic clinics: pediatric neurology. Philadelphia: WB Saunders, 1985:77–94.

Hockaday J, Barlow CF. Headache in children. In: (eds) The headaches. New York: Raven Press, 1993:795–808.

Rosenberger PB. Headaches. In: (eds) Pediatric neurology for the clinician. New York: Appleton and Lange, 1992:547–556.

Rothner DA. Headache in the pediatric and adolescent population. In: (eds) Headache diagnosis and treatment. Baltimore: Williams & Wilkins, 1993:271–279.

Rothner DA. Management of headaches in children and adolescents. J Pain Sympt Manage 1993; 8:2–8.

Slillito P, Stephenson J. Headaches in children: action or reassurance. Practitioner 1994; 238.

Supplementary Search Strategy

SuSS I	
Subject	explode Headache (index term) or headache (text word)
Subject	explode Child (index term)
Limited to	1994 through 1997

Chapter 17

Migraine in Women

Migraine occurs in females three times more frequently than in males after puberty. In childhood the prevalence is the same in both sexes. Throughout a woman's life there can be fluctuations in hormones for a variety of reasons. Migraines can be affected by the changes that begin with menarche and end with menopause.

MENSTRUAL MIGRAINE

Menstrual migraine is defined as migraine which occurs on day one of the menstrual cycle +/- 2 days, with the remainder of the cycle being headache free. This occurs in only 8 to 10% of women, whereas migraineurs who experience an exacerbation around the time of menstruation represent the majority (60%).

The headache is typical of migraine experienced at other times of the month: severe throbbing headache associated with nausea, vomiting, photophobia, with or without aura, lasting a few days to a week. The trigger in menstrual migraine appears to be an abrupt drop in estrogen prior to the onset of menses.

Treatment of menstrual migraine follows the same principles as those established for the management of migraine (see Chapter 8, *Migraine*).

Once again treatment may be abortive or preventive. Over-the-counter analgesics such as aspirin and acetaminophen may be used if headache severity is mild and if the patient responds well to these drugs. Prescription abortive treatments include sumatriptan (Imitrex), dihydroergotamine (DHE), and ergotamine preparations. Although there are few conclusive trials, many other approaches may be tried.

If the migraines occur at a predictable time in the cycle, nonsteroidal anti-inflammatory drugs (NSAIDs) may be prescribed 3 to 4 days premenstrually and for the duration of the menses in an attempt to prevent or minimize the attack. Since menstrual migraine is believed to result, at least in part, from the immediate

Critical Decisions

A Abortive treatment
- Abortive treatment for migraine includes OTC analgesia, antiemetics, or NSAIDs.

B Preventive treatment
- Preventive treatment should be considered if the above fails. If migraine occurs at a predictable time in the cycle, medication (NSAID) may be given 2-4 days prior.
- If headache occurrence is not predictable, consider migraine prevention.

C Severe menstrual migraine
- Severe menstrual migraine can be treated in the same method as "migraine" with specific antimigraine drugs.

D Hormone therapy
- Menstrual migraine is thought to occur as a result of a drop in plasma estradiol. Therefore, hormone manipulation may be an effective mode of treatment.

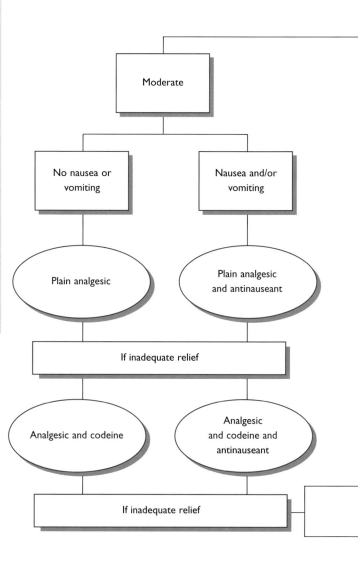

Treatment of Menstrual Migraine

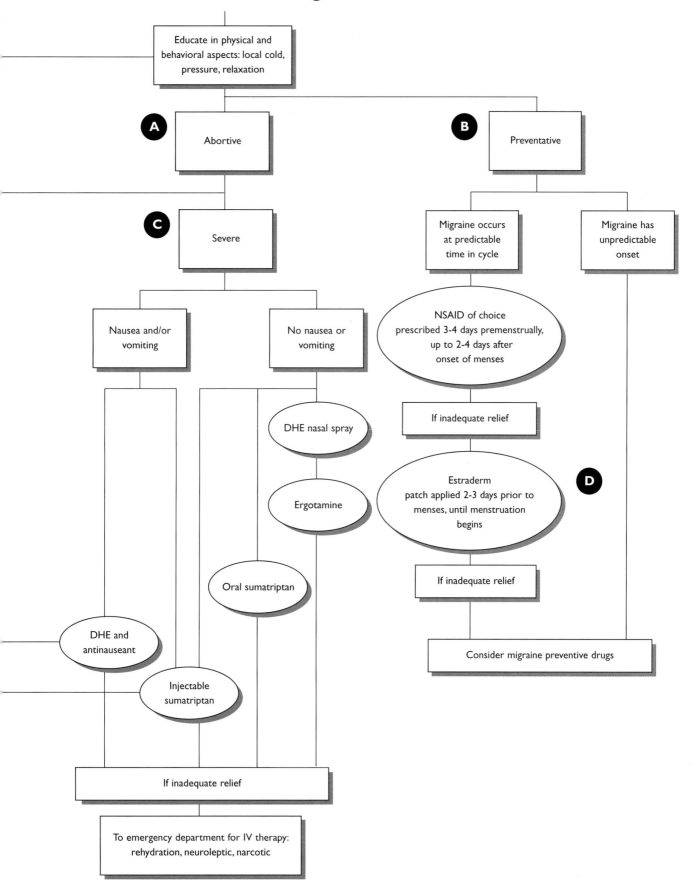

premenstrual drop in plasma estradiol, administration of supplemental estrogens can be quite effective. An estradiol patch (Estraderm) may be applied 2 to 3 days prior to the expected onset of menses and changes on days -1 and +1 for a total of three patches per cycle. Occasionally, NSAIDs and estrogen are given for longer periods of time, with better effect on menstrual migraine, but it must be remembered that both these treatments have side effects which may become more likely with prolonged treatment.

BIRTH CONTROL PILL

The association of migraine with the birth control pill remains controversial with a variety of studies reporting conflicting results. Migraine attacks have been shown to change in character, increase, decrease, or remain unchanged while the migraineur is on the birth control pill, depending on the study cited. When migraines do increase with use of the birth control pill, a majority occur in a drug-free interval (ie, while off estrogen for a few days each month). The frequency of headache may escalate anywhere from the first month up to a year after the pill is started. Migraines may occur for the first time on the birth control pill and may or may not decrease after the pill has been discontinued.

The risk of stroke in migraineurs may be slightly higher; if the migraineur is taking the birth control pill, the risk may be even higher, possibly as a consequence of increased serum estrogen levels, producing a hypercoagulable state. Therefore, when prescribing birth control pills to a migraine sufferer, the physician should consider a low dose estrogen preparation. The physician should also exercise caution when prescribing the birth control pill to a migraineur with a history of smoking, which also increases the risk of stroke.

Treatment of migraine occurring on the birth control pill should follow the same principles as that of acute migraine treatment (see Chapter 8, *Migraine*). If the patient and physician choose to continue the birth control pill, the headaches can be treated with the usual avoidance of triggers and with abortive therapy, including analgesics, sumatriptan, ergotamine, and DHE. If the headaches do not subside with the usual antimigraine therapy, consideration should be given to discontinuing the use of the birth control pill.

Although migraine is not an absolute contraindication to the birth control pill, the physician should be alert to any changes in the pattern of the headache while the patient is on the pill. Worsening severity, increasing frequency or severe sudden onset of headache, and especially the development of any new neurologic symptoms or aura in association with the headache should prompt discontinuation of the pill and initiation of an investigation with computed tomography (CT) scans or magnetic resonance imaging (MRI) to exclude subarachnoid hemorrhage or cerebral vessel thrombosis. These conditions are known to mimic migraine clinically in people. Combined oral contraceptive pills are contraindicted in patients with migraine with aura and in migraineurs with other vascular risk factors (smoking, hypertension, etc.).

MIGRAINE IN PREGNANCY

Migraines may be affected in a variety of ways by pregnancy: they may increase, diminish, or remain unchanged. Headaches may also appear for the first time during pregnancy, usually during the first trimester, and typically subside in the second and third trimesters. Often migraines recur in the postpartum period and may be associated with depression. Frequently, women whose migraines began with menarche and are linked to menses, may experience relief of headache during pregnancy.

When headaches occur during pregnancy, the possibility of cerebral vein thrombosis and subarachnoid hemorrhage should be considered in the differential diagnoses, especially if the headaches are sudden and severe in their onset. Once more sinister causes have been eliminated, treatment of migraine in pregnancy raises a dilemma, owing to the risk of teratogenic effects and potential effects on the course of the pregnancy itself. The physician should consult and work closely with the obstetrician in determining appropriate therapies. Ideally, nonpharmacologic approaches should be considered first, including elimination of triggers, adoption of a proper diet, behavior modification, relaxation therapy, ice packs, and massage. If the headache frequency and severity increases to the extent where the baby's well-being is being threatened, medical management should be initiated. If dehydration has occurred secondary to excessive vomiting, fluid replacement should be given. The patient must be told of any potential risk associated with the drugs prior to their administration.

Acetaminophen can usually be given without teratogenic effects; however, narcotics and codeine should be avoided and used with caution to avoid potential addiction in the baby and the mother. Aspirin should be avoided due to its effect on coagulation in both fetus and mother in later stages of pregnancy. NSAIDs may inhibit labor. Antimigraine therapy including sumatriptan and ergotamine preparations are contraindicated in pregnancy. If preventive treatment is indicated for refractory headache with associated severe vomiting and dehydration, then a low dose beta-blocker or a tricyclic antidepressant could be tried. Although there have been reports of intrauterine growth retardation there are no known teratogenic effects associated with beta-blockers.

MENOPAUSE

Although the frequency of migraines may decrease with age, there may be an increase just prior to or during menopause. Hormone replacement therapy (HRT) used in menopause may either relieve or exacerbate the headaches. Treatment of headaches during menopause may be problematic. It may be difficult to determine whether the underlying cause of the headaches is from menopause or its hormone treatment. Also, it may not be possible to discontinue HRT if this is the underlying cause of headaches. The usual migraine therapies may be tried initially. Alternatively, manipulation of HRT could be attempted in a variety of ways: (a) reduce the estrogen dosage, (b) change hormone replacement therapy from interrupted to continuous, (c) change the route of administration from oral to parenteral, (d) consider adding androgen, and (e) change the estrogen preparation.

Bibliography

Bousser M, Massiou H. Migraine in the reproductive cycle. In: Olesen J, Tfelt-Hanson P, Welch K, eds. The Headaches. New York: Raven Press, 1993:413–420.

Silberstein S. Migraine and women. Postgrad Med 1995; 97:147–153.

Silberstein S, Merriam GR. Estrogens, progestins and headache. Neurology 1991; 41:786–793.

Welch K. Migraine and pregnancy. Adv Neurol 1994; 64:77–81.

Supplementary Search Strategies

SuSS 1

Subject	Migraine (index term) or migraine (text word)
Subject	explode Contraceptive Agents, Female (index term))
Limited to	1994 through 1997

SuSS 2

Subject	Migraine (mh) or migraine (text word)
Subject	explode Menstrual Cycle (index term) or menstrua: (text word)
Limited to	1994 through 1997

SuSS 3

Subject	Migraine (index term) or migraine (text word)
Subject	explode Pregnancy (index term)
Limited to	1994 through 1997

SuSS 4

Subject	Migraine (mh) or migraine (text word)
Subject	explode Climacteric (index term) or menopaus: (index term)
Limited to	1994 through 1997

Chapter 18

Headache in The Elderly

Headache in the elderly presents a special challenge to the physician. The clinician not only faces a perplexing variety of etiologies for headaches, but also contends with the difficulty of managing headache where associated conditions may contraindicate and complicate treatment decisions.

Although headache is an important source of morbidity in the aged, the actual incidence of headache declines with age; however, it still may be a marker of a serious underlying disorder. The possibility of other underlying medical or possibly serious structural disorders must be included in the differential diagnosis in this population. Although headache disorders from earlier years may continue into the later years of life, any change in pattern of the headache and particularly new onset headache must be evaluated to rule out the possibility of associated underlying disease.

Headache in the elderly may be divided into primary headache, including migraine, cluster, and tension headache; and secondary headache, including intracranial masses, hemorrhage, infection, and metabolic disease. Only after secondary causes have been excluded should treatment be considered for possible primary headaches.

PRIMARY HEADACHE

Tension Headache

As in the younger population, tension headaches are frequently described as mild to moderate, bilateral tightening pressure-like headaches whose intensity may vary; however, usually the headache does not limit the patient's physical activity. The clinical examination is normal. The differential diagnosis of tension headache should include cervicogenic headache, migraine, mass lesion, ophthalmologic conditions (e.g., glaucoma), and temporal arteritis.

In treating tension headaches nonpharmacologic approaches should be considered, such as physical therapy, massage, and local heat application. The possibility of an underlying depression should also be considered as an associated condition. Tricyclic antidepressants may be used for medical management, but caution should be exercised owing to the potential side effects, especially in the elderly patient with prostatism or glaucoma. Underlying cardiac disease and particularly cardiac arrhythmias may also contraindicate treatment with tricyclic antidepressants. Nonsteroidal anti-inflammatory medications (NSAIDs) may be a reasonable alternative, but again patients should be evaluated frequently for the possibility of associated renal failure or gastric irritation.

Migraine

Although onset of migraine is unusual in the elderly, it can certainly be carried on from youth. Frequently, migraines will diminish with age although they may persist. The description of the migraines in the elderly is similar to that in a younger population: The headache is typically unilateral or bitemporal with a throbbing component; it is frequently associated with nausea, vomiting, and photophobia; and it may be accompanied by aura. Some headaches may be caused by the common triggers (see Chapter 8, *Migraine*).

In the elderly, especially, the transient migraine equivalents described by Fisher must be distinguished from transient ischemic attacks. These migraine equivalents are episodes of transient neurologic dysfunction, with or without headache, featuring such symptoms as transient global amnesia, vertigo, scintillating scotoma, or hemisensory loss. These patients should be investigated to rule out the possibility of transient ischemic attack before a diagnosis of migraine equivalent is considered.

Treatment of migraine should be approached as it is in the younger population, but with several precautions. Coronary artery disease, hypertension, angina, and peripheral vascular disease may preclude treatment with ergotamine, sumatriptan, and methysergide. Patients with prostatism, arrhythmia, or glaucoma should avoid the tricyclic antidepressants. Beta-blockers may be contraindicated in patients with congestive heart failure, obstructive pulmonary diseases, and diabetes.

In situations where hypertension coexists with migraine, treatment with a beta-blocker or calcium-blocking agent may be useful. In the elderly there are certain factors which may in fact aggravate migraine, such as hypertension.

Vasodilators used in the treatment of ischemic heart disease may also act as exacerbators. Similarly, estrogen used to treat postmenopausal women may exacerbate migraine.

Even without obvious contraindications, with certain medications used to treat migraine in the elderly, side effects may occur more frequently. Medications should be introduced cautiously—"start low and go slow."

Cluster Headache

Typically, these headaches occur between the ages of 20 and 50. They are characterized by unilateral orbital or temporal pain, lasting 15 minutes to 3 hours. They may occur several times during the course of the day. There may be associated lacrimation, conjunctivitis, rhinitis, miosis, and ptosis on the same side as the pain. Although these symptoms may occur for the first time in the elderly, other underlying conditions should be excluded. The differential diagnoses should include glaucoma, carotid dissection, mass lesion, and the effect of medication such as vasodilators. As with younger patients, treatment of cluster headache consists of oxygen inhalation, sumatriptan, ergotamine, lithium, verapamil, or prednisone (see Chapter 8).

SECONDARY HEADACHE

Structural Lesions

In the geriatric patient, any new onset headache or change in the previous pattern of headache should be considered a possible space-occupying lesion until proven otherwise.

Space-occupying lesions to be considered include tumors of primary or secondary type or subdural hematomas. Primary tumors in this age group include glioma, meningioma, or pituitary adenoma. The most common secondary metastatic tumors are from melanoma, and from primary lesions of lung, breast, kidney, or large bowel.

A headache that occurs with subdural hematoma may be very similar to that associated with a tumor, and may occur with or without focal signs. The pain may not be localized. A subdural hematoma may occur with or without a history of trauma. They may also be associated with a more gradual onset of nonspecific symptoms including dizziness, cognitive changes, drowsiness, and subtle personality changes.

Although headaches associated mass lesions are often nonspecific, they may exhibit features characteristic of raised intracranial pressure, including awakening the patient during the night, nausea and vomiting, and aggravation by exertion.

Ischemic Cerebrovascular Disease

It is not widely known that cerebral ischemia, whether fleeting (TIA.) or lasting ("stroke") is associated with headaches in about 25% of cases. Their pathogenesis is unknown. These headaches may accompany the ischemic event, causing it to mimic a cerebral hemorrhage. More importantly, they may precede the ischemic event by hours, days, or sometimes weeks—thus giving warning that something is amiss in the cerebral circulation and allowing an opportunity for preventive action. Recognizing them is the problem.

Usually they are ipsilateral to the ischemia, throbbing, not very severe, and last minutes to hours. There is nothing specific about them, but they should be regarded as suspicious if only because they are new headaches occurring for the first time in or after middle age.

When the ischemia is caused by blatant carotid disease such as dissection or total occlusion, there may be an ipsilateral Horner's syndrome (meiosis and ptosis), but these situations are rare, and usually there are no clues on the physical examination to suggest that something ominous is brewing.

Hemorrhagic Cerebrovascular Disease

Intracerebral hemorrhage is usually easy to diagnose; the headache is associated with a clear-cut focal lesion and, in the larger hemorrhages, signs of increased intracranial pressure such as obtundation and vomiting. Subarachnoid hemorrhage is not difficult to diagnose when large, but can be tricky when small, because they may present only with headache and perhaps some neck stiffness (see Chapter 15, *Emergency Management of Acute Headache*). Even these, however, can be recognized if one always remembers to view new headaches with onset after the age of 45 or 50 with great suspicion.

High Blood Pressure

The idea that mild to moderate high blood pressure causes headache is incorrect. Most hypertensive individuals with headaches have the same migraine and tension-type headaches that afflict their normotensive brethren. Only severe hypertension (diastolic blood pressure >120 mmHg) is likely to cause headache. Usually this is long-sustained hypertension, but a sudden acute increase in blood pressure (such as occurs when taking cocaine or amphetamines, when patients on monoamine oxidase inhibitors take sympathomimetic medications, or with a pheochromocytoma) may produce sudden, intense bursting headache that then persists for hours and may culminate in intracerebral hemorrhage.

Temporal Arteritis

Temporal arteritis is a treatable condition and should be considered in any patient over age 60 presenting with unilateral headaches (see Chapter 11, *Inflammatory Headaches*).

Examination may reveal tenderness and induration of the superficial temporal artery with a diminished pulse. Visual acuity and fields should be examined for evidence of impairment. Although the erythrocyte sedimentation rate (ESR) is generally elevated in this condition, a normal value does not exclude a diagnosis of temporal arteritis; if the clinical history and physical examination are consistent with a diagnosis of temporal arteritis, biopsy should be pursued in spite of a normal ESR.

Headache Associated with Systemic Disease

According to the description provided by the International Headache Society, metabolic headache is that which occurs during metabolic disturbance and disappears within seven days after normalization of the disruption. Because of the comorbidity of other conditions in the geriatric population, consideration should be given to causes including infection, hypertension, hypercarbia, sleep apnea, and underlying malignancy, whenever a patient presents with new onset headache.

A number of metabolic and systemic diseases can cause headache in the elderly. The main subcategories will be discussed briefly.

Hypoxic headaches may be seen in a number of settings including headache associated with reduced ambient oxygen levels. Much more likely in the geriatric population, hypoxic headaches are associated with primary pulmonary disease, cardiac failure, and anemia. Hypoxia produces cerebral vasodilation, which in turn causes headache.

Hypercapnia (carbon dioxide greater than 50 mmHg) should be considered when headaches are generalized, pounding, present on awakening, and improve as the patient gets up and moves around. These headaches clinically may be indistinguishable from some others except that they respond to correction of the hypercapnia.

Anemia when severe may be associated with a dull diffuse headache, again produced by cerebral vasodilation.

Other metabolic derangements, including chronic renal failure and dialysis, can produce chronic headache in this elderly population.

As in the general population, *hypoglycemia* may produce headaches, or exacerbate pre-existing headaches. These headaches may be moderate to severe, may be associated with nausea, and in some cases may clinically resemble migraine in their description.

In the elderly, *acute closed-angle glaucoma* may frequently be associated with orbitofrontal headaches. Clinical examination may reveal an irregular light reflex, or a fixed mildly dilated pupil, or most importantly, a "red eye" ("white eyes" are *rarely* a cause of headache). The findings should prompt immediate referral to an ophthalmologist.

Trigeminal Neuralgia

These "headaches" are described as brief, severe, electrical shock-like paroxysms of unilateral pain in the distribution of the second and/or third divisions of the trigeminal nerve. They are in fact seldom described as "headaches," but rather as "pain in the face." Triggering the pain by touching the face is an important diagnostic pointer. In the elderly, trigeminal neuralgia may be secondary to microvascular compression of the trigeminal nerve root. Treatment includes carbomazepine, and sometimes lioresal. Caution should be exercised in using these medications in this elderly population owing to the potential side effects of drowsiness and dizziness (see Chapter 12, *Cranial Neuralgias and Facial Pain,* for details.)

Medication-Induced Headache

These headaches are usually bifrontal in location and constant in nature. A careful review of all the patient's medications at frequent intervals is essential in identifying and eliminating those which either are unnecessary or may be contributing to headaches. Common medications used in the elderly which are associated with headache include nitrates, hydralazine, nifedipine, estrogen, and nonsteroidal anti-inflammatories. Over-the-counter medications such as NSAIDs, and ergotamine, and analgesic compounds have also been implicated in medication-induced headaches (see Chapter 14, *Medication-Induced Headache*).

Headaches Associated with Neck Disease

Cervical spondylosis is more common with aging and is said to represent a common cause of headache in the elderly. The features of "cervicogenic headache" include occipital pain and limitation in range of motion of the neck, and muscle spasm of the cervical muscles. Associated abnormalities may be detected by physical examination of structures in the cervical root distribution, including sensory deficits, reflex changes, or muscle wasting in the arms. These headaches may be particularly distressing to the elderly and represent a challenging therapeutic problem. Treatment with medication may be limited, although simple analgesics, such as ASA, acetaminophen or NSAIDs, may be tried in conjunction with a mild muscle relaxant. Other approaches such as physiotherapy and massage treatments should also be considered.

Summary

Headache in the elderly may resemble those of the younger population. However, new onset headache or a change in the previous pattern of headache warrants a careful search for the possibility of associated structural and systemic disease. Treatment of headaches in the elderly may be complicated by comorbidity of other conditions and by the sensitivity of older people to side effects of medications.

Table 18.1   Headache in the Elderly

Primary	Secondary
Tension	Tumor
	Primary
	Metastatic
Migraine	Bleeding
	Subdural
	Intracranial
	Subarachnoid
Cluster	Cerebrovascular disease
	Temporal arteritis
	Systemic disease
	Trigeminal neuralgia
	Medication-induced
	Headache associated with ear, nose, throat, neck, and cranium

Critical Decisions

(A) **Headache in the elderly**
- Although headache incidence declines with age, in the elderly it may be a marker of a severe underlying medical disorder.
- Change in pattern of headache, or new onset must be evaluated.

(B) **Migraine**
- Onset of migraine in the elderly is unusual, but has a presentation similar to that of the younger population.
- Migraine equivalent may mimic transient ischemic attacks (TIA), or TIA may mimic migraine.

(C) **Underlying pathology**
- Cerebrovascular disease may cause unilateral throbbing headache, lateralized to the side of ischemia.
- Headache can be associated with hemorrhage, ischemia, or infarction.
- Headache associated with stroke may be mild and nonthrobbing, and may occur before, during, or after stroke.

(D) **Temporal arteritis**
- Headache of temporal arteritis is associated with tenderness and induration of the superficial temporal artery.
- ESR is usually elevated, but a normal value does not exclude the diagnosis, and a biopsy should be considered.

(E) **Medication-induced headache**
- Common medications used by the elderly that may induce headache include nitrates, hydralazine, nifedipine, estrogen and NSAIDs.

A **Evaluating Headache in The Elderly** (part 1)

Headaches occur daily/almost daily

Attacks last a few hours to all day

Multiple brief (< 2 hours) attacks every day

Headaches: Unilateral or bilateral, pulsatile or nonpulsatile, more severe ones may be associated with nausea and/or vomiting

Headaches: Nonlateralized and/or no tearing, or rhinorrhea, etc, and/or lancinating

Headaches: Consistently lateralized, predominantly periocular, associated with tearing and rhinorrhea

No other symptoms

Other neurologic or systemic symptoms

Other symptoms

No other symptoms

B Normal examination

Abnormal examination

Normal examination

Normal or abnormal examination

Normal examination (except for Horner's syndrome ipsilateral to pain)

Medication overuse

Suspect presence of lesion, neurologic consultation, investigate

Suspect presence of lesion, neurologic consultation, investigate

Chronic tension-type headache or tension-migraine

Major possibilities: intracranial mass lesion, hydrocephalus, or "benign" intracranial hypertension (BIH), vasculitis, smouldering meningitis, metabolic, craniovertebral lesions, sinusitis.

C

D

Major possibilities: lesion near base of brain, post fossa lesion.

Suspect medication-induced headache

E

Procedures: CT scan or MRI, systemic investigation for metabolic disease, lumbar puncture, others as indicated.

Cluster headaches or one of its variants

Procedures: CT scan or MRI, others as indicated.

Critical Decisions

A Headache in the elderly
- Although headache incidence declines with age, in the elderly it may be a marker of a severe underlying medical disorder.
- Change in pattern of headache, or new onset must be evaluated.

B Migraine
- Onset of migraine in the elderly is unusual, but has a presentation similar to that of the younger population.
- Migraine may mimic transient ischemic attacks (TIA) and TIA may mimic migraine.

C Underlying pathology
- Cerebrovascular disease may cause unilateral throbbing headache, lateralized to the side of ischemia.
- Headache may be associated with hemorrhage, ischemia, or infarction.
- Headache associated with stroke may be mild and non-throbbing, and may occur before, during, or after stroke.

D Temporal arteritis
- Headache of temporal arteritis is associated with tenderness and induration of the superficial temporal artery.
- ESR is usually elevated, but a normal value does not exclude the diagnosis, and a biopsy should be considered.

Headaches: Hemicranial or bilateral, aggravated by physical activity, pulsatility, accompanied by nausea/vomiting, accompanied by phonophotophobia, preceded by typical visual aura

No other symptoms

Other neurologic or systemic symptoms

Normal examination

Abnormal examination

Normal or abnormal examination

B Migraine

Suspect presence of lesion, neurologic consultation, investigate

Procedures: CT scan or MRI, angiography as indicated, others as indicated

Major possibilities: Intracranial mass, vasculitis, temporal arteritis, cerebrovascular disease

C
D

A Evaluating Headache in The Elderly (part 2)

Episodic

Recurrent attacks: Duration of few hours to days; frequency every few days for several weeks

Headaches: Bilateral, unaffected by physical activity, nonpulsatile, no accompaniments

No other symptoms

Abnormal examination

Normal examination

Tension-type headache

Fulminant

Isolated violent headache lasting hours to weeks

Headaches: Rapid to abrupt onset, extraordinary intensity, associated prostration

Considered ominous unless all of the following are present: No other symptoms except nausea and/or vomiting, perfectly normal examination, headache improving spontaneously, previous identical headaches with benign outcome

All the above criteria **are** met

All the above criteria are **not** met

B Severe migraine

Suspect presence of lesion, neurologic consultation, investigate

C

Procedures: CT scan or MRI, lumbar puncture, others as indicated

Major possibilities: Subarachnoid hemorrhage, meningoencephalitis, cerebral hemorrhage, intracranial mass lesion, arterial dissection, cerebrovascular disease

Bibliography

Baumel B, Eisner L. Diagnosis and treatment of headache in the elderly. Med Clin North Am 1991; 75:661–675.

Bogousslasky J, Regli F, et al. Migraine stroke. Neurology 1988; 38:223–227.

Dalessio J, ed. Wolff's headache and other head pain (5th ed.). New York: Oxford University Press, 1987:494–495.

Edmeads J, Takahashi A. Headache in the elderly. In: Olesen J, ed. The headaches. New York: Raven Press, 1993:809–813.

Elkind A. Headache in a geriatric population. In: Tollison CD, Kunkel RS, eds. Headache diagnosis and treatment. (5th ed.). Baltimore: Williams & Wilkins, 1993:281–288.

Fisher CM. Late life migraine accompaniments as a cause of unexplained transient ischemic attacks. Can J Neurol Sci 1980; 7:9–18.

Kaminski HJ, Ruff RL. Treatment of the elderly patient with headache or trigeminal neuralgia. Drugs Aging 1991; 1:48–56.

Lipton RB, et al. Headaches in the elderly. Pain Symptom Management 1993; 8:87–97.

Supplementary Search Strategies

SuSS 1

Subject	Tension Headache (index term)
Limited to	explode aged (index term)
AND	1994 through 1997

SuSS 2

Subject	Migraine (index term) or migraine (text word)
Limited to	Aged or 80 and over
AND	1994 through 1997

SuSS 3

Subject	Cluster Headache (index term)
Limited to	Aged or 80 and over
AND	1994 through 1997

INDEX

**December 2007
Caroline Roberts**
Editorial

2007—How was it for us?

Welcome to the biggest edition of Grafik ever. As usual we've packed out the issue with the very best things from the past year. We'd like to thank all of our contributors and everyone who has sent us their work—we had so much good stuff that even if we had a 300-page magazine we'd be struggling to fit it all in.

It's been another great year for the mag—as well as all of the usual graphic design-related shenanigans there have been several new additions to Team Grafik (hello, Stefan; hello, Danny), many more speciality teas (hello, Mssrs Birt & Tang), even more top-class biscuits (hello, Mr Bahlsen), the first ever Grafik cleaner (hello, Hristina) and, most importantly, the first Grafik baby (hello, Jacob).

Grafik's already looking forward to 2008, and all the optimism (once the Resolve's kicked in) that a New Year brings. According to Chinese astrology, 2008 is the year of the rat. While rats are pretty low down the pecking order in the West, in Eastern mythology the rat is not a creature to be trifled with—in fact, it is ranked number one in the calendar of twelve animals.

Being a water sign means that the rat is very powerful—when faced with a snake or a horse it will always win. The rat's weasel-like qualities mean that it can overpower a snake, but you may be wondering how a rat could possibly overcome a horse? Simple, really: if the horse eats rat droppings it dies. There's a moral in there, and maybe those of you who are still looking for a New Year's resolution could do worse than adopt this one: to never, ever underestimate the power of shifty-looking brown rodents, and under no circumstances eat their poo.

Happy New Year from everyone at Grafik.